STUDIES IN SPENSER'S HISTORICAL ALLEGORY

JOHNS HOPKINS MONOGRAPHS IN LITERARY HISTORY
II

STUDIES IN SPENSER'S HISTORICAL ALLEGORY

BY

EDWIN GREENLAW

1967

OCTAGON BOOKS, INC.

New York

Reprinted 1967
by special arrangement with The Johns Hopkins Press

OCTAGON BOOKS, INC.
175 FIFTH AVENUE
NEW YORK, N. Y. 10010

LIBRARY OF CONGRESS CATALOG CARD NUMBER: 67-18763

Printed in U.S.A. by
NOBLE OFFSET PRINTERS, INC.
NEW YORK 3, N. Y.

TO

DOROTHY, MARGERY, AND MARY

PREFACE

This volume consists of four papers of the late Professor Greenlaw, the first two not before published. Chapter I was read before the History of Ideas Club at The Johns Hopkins University, December 15, 1927, and later at the annual meeting of the Modern Language Association at Louisville in the same year. Chapter II represents material used in the English Conference and Seminary at Hopkins and read as the presidential address before The Johns Hopkins Philological Association in October, 1929. Chapter III is a reprint of Professor Greenlaw's article, "Spenser and the Earl of Leicester," from *Publications of the Modern Language Association* 25 (1910), 535-561; and Chapter IV is a reprint of his "Spenser and British Imperialism" from *Modern Philology* 9 (1912), 347-370.

Although Professor Greenlaw had not changed any of his opinions regarding the fundamental theses of the two articles here reprinted, he intended, nevertheless, to revise them before including them in this work. Had he been able to carry out this revision, he would, I am sure, have modified some details and strengthened others, and he would have taken into account the criticisms that have been made of the articles in question. Obviously, I could do none of this. I have, therefore, printed them just as he left them.

PREFACE

The Commentary is made up from his notes, which I have arranged and to which I have added a few illustrations. I have placed in the Commentary many notes which Professor Greenlaw collected for inclusion in the text, but I did not feel free to insert them there. I have supplied some of the references and checked those cited by Professor Greenlaw.

Mrs. Greenlaw has made possible the publication of this volume not only by supplying all MSS and notes, but also by her generous financial aid for the printing. I wish to thank the editors of *Publications of the Modern Language Association* and *Modern Philology* for permission to reprint the articles named above, and the editor of *Studies in Philology* for permission to include in the Commentary a section of Professor Greenlaw's "Spenser's Fairy Mythology" from volume 15 (1918). I am indebted to Professor Kemp Malone, Dr. James G. McManaway, and Dr. Ernest A. Strathmann for their assistance in reading all the proofs.

I cannot end this preface without expressing my gratitude for the rare privilege of having been associated with Professor Greenlaw as his student and assistant. My debt to him is large, and I am happy that I have been able to do the small service of preparing for the press one of his books, in partial repayment for his many kindnesses. Repayment in full I could never make.

RAY HEFFNER

Baltimore, April, 1932

CONTENTS

————

ix

CHAPTER ONE

The Battle of the Books

I labour to pourtraict in Arthure, before he was king, the image of a brave knight, perfected in the twelve private morall vertues . . . which if I finde to be well accepted, I may be perhaps encoraged to frame the other part of polliticke vertues in his person, after that hee came to be king . . . I conceive (Prince Arthur) after his long education by Timon . . . to have seene in a dream or vision the Faery Queen, with whose excellent beauty ravished, he awaking resolved to seeke her out, and so being by Merlin armed, and by Timon throughly instructed, he went to seeke her forth in Faerye land. In that Faery Queene I meane glory in my generall intention, but in my particular I conceive the most excellent and glorious person on our soveraine the Queene, and her kingdome in Faery land . . . So in the person of Prince Arthure I sette forth magnificence in particular . . . For the Methode of a Poet historical is not such as of an Historiographer. For an Historiographer discourseth of affayres orderly as they were donne, accounting as well the times as the actions; but a Poet thrusteth into the middest, even where it most concerneth him, and then recoursing to the thinges forepaste, and divining of thinges to come, maketh a pleasing Analysis of all.

Full understanding of Spenser's theme in the *Faerie Queene* depends upon a battle of the books which began in the early Tudor period and persisted, in various forms, until the accession of a new dynasty. While the glorification of the House of Tudor has long been recognized as one element in Spenser's poem, the structural

1

importance of the theme has been singularly neglected. Furthermore, the theme has been regarded as his own invention, in imitation of Vergil and Ariosto. But Spenser, like Shakespeare, invented little. His praise of the Tudor house was no mere literary compliment nor a trick of epic technique. It was the expression of a philosophy of history, of a conception of British destiny. He did not invent it, but found it ready to his hand in a score of places. He glorified it, so that it became part of the structure itself of the greatest work of the imagination produced during the Elizabethan period. That he looked upon himself as an historical poet, aiming at the interpretation of English history though using a method different from that of an historiographer; that he was an antiquary moved by the same spirit as that which animated the noble group of students of Britain's past; that the historical portions of the poem are clues to its meaning, not mere intrusions of old work into the romance, are all matters of importance. A study of these matters will not only bring into the circle of influences on Spenser's mind and art a large and interesting group of sources but will also point the way to the proper interpretation of his continued or historical allegory.

I

In 1534 Polydore Vergil's *Anglicae Historiae Libri xxvi* was published. Its author, born at Urbino, educated at Padua and Bologna, and for some years in the service of the Duke of Urbino and of Alexander VI, came to England about 1501. He attained high favor with Henry VII, who commissioned him to write a history of England; he held various offices, including that of archdeacon at Wells, near Glastonbury, in the Arthur country; he was on friendly terms with Fox, More, Linacre, and Latimer, and, with some intermissions, with Erasmus; after a few years he became naturalized as a British subject; he quarreled with Wolsey and for a short time was in prison, to the great scandal of his Italian friends; late in life he returned to Italy, where he died some twenty years after his chief work, the History, had appeared.

Though naturalized, Polydore appears to have remained at heart an Italian of the Renaissance. He disputed with Erasmus concerning the priority of their respective collections of *Adagia*. The quarrel was made up, and he even offered, at one time, to assist Erasmus with money, but he re-iterated his claim in later editions of his book. He was little at Wells, and though he presented some hangings for the choir, with his arms, which his opponent Leland duly registered in his *Itinerary*, he sold the archdeacon's house, when he departed, with doubtful propriety. He did not choose to further Wolsey's ambition to wear the Cardinal's hat, and his account of Wolsey, in his History, shows the prejudice which he maintained an historian should avoid. He was an Italian Catholic; he did not sympathize with the liberal movement in the English church; he hated the Britons and preferred the Saxons; but he wrote an excellent history and he precipitated a conflict of far-reaching importance.

Polydore's history differs from chronicles of the earlier type in that he fuses his material into a connected narrative and applies canons of criticism to his authorities. He anticipates Bacon in his theory that it is the office of the historian to present facts as best he can ascertain them and to allow the reader to draw his own conclusions. He professes to avoid prejudice. " It is a law in history," he says, " that the writer should never be so bold as to open any false things, nor so demisse as not to utter any truth." He regarded contemporary testimony, as of Bede, as competent, and in response to criticism on a certain point asserted that it would not be lawful for him to intermeddle by reason of the law incumbent upon an historian not to refrain from the revelation of falsehood nor to give suspicion of favor or envy. He wrote to James IV for information concerning Scottish kings; James refused on the ground that he could not expect an impartial account from a foreigner; Polydore secured his information from other sources.

It was this critical judgment of authorities and decision to seek, so far as possible, for first-hand information that led him to reject Geoffrey of Monmouth's account of Arthur and of the deeds of the Britons. Gildas he deemed competent, and he praised his predecessor for telling the truth about his countrymen. But he was not content with rejecting the legends concerning the descent of the Britons from Troy and the Arthurian matter. Speed, nearly a century later, did the same thing, and did it thoroughly, though with better manners. Polydore argues for Gildas in the following terms:

It is noe smalle argumente of his [Gildas'] synceritee that in uttering the trewthe he spareth not his owne nation, and, wheare as he speakethe littell good of his contriemenne, he beewailethe manie eevels in them, nether dothe he feare in revealinge the troth thoughe he were a Britton, to write of Brittons that thei nether weare stoute in battayle nor faithefull in peace.

And he continues, with a repetition of William of Newburgh's attack on Geoffrey:

But on the other side there hathe appaered a writer in owre time which, to purge these defaultes of Brittains, feininge of them thinges to be laughed at, hathe extolled them aboove the noblenes of Romains and Macedonians, enhauncinge them with most imprudent lyeing. This man is cauled Geffray, sur-named Arthure, bie cause that owte of the olde lesings of Brittons, being somwhat augmented bie him, hee hathe recited manie things of this King Arthure, taking unto him bothe the coloure of Latin speeche and the honest pretext of an Historie: more over, taking in hande a greater enterprice, he hathe pub-lished the sowthsaiengs of one Merlin, as prophesies of most assuered and approved trewthe, allways addinge somwhat of his own while translatethe them into Latine. This saithe he [adds Polydore], Gildas before him, but not I, which write nothing but that which hathe ben written beefore, wherefore there is noe man which justlie can be angrie with mee for this sainge (that thei were nether valiaunte in battaile nether true in leage), which was a reproche to the owld Britons.

His account of Arthur is in the same strain:

At this time Utherius departed owte of this world, after whome succeded his sonne Arthur, being noe doubte suche a mann as, if hee had lived longe, hee surelie woulde have restored the whole somme beeinge allmost loste to his Britons. As concerninge this noble prince, for the marvelus force of his boddie, and the invincible valiaunce of his minde, his posteritee hathe allmoste vaunted and divulged suche gestes, as in our memorie amonge the Italiens ar commonlie noysed of Roland, the nephew of Charles the Great bie his sister, allbeit hee perished in the floure of his yowthe; for the common people is at this presence soe affectioned, that with wonderus admiration they extol Arthure unto the heavens, alleginge that hee daunted three capitans of the Saxons in plaine feelde; that hee subdewed Scotlande with the Iles adjoyninge; that in the teritorie of the Parisiens hee manfullie overthrew the Romaines, with there capitan Lucius, that hee didd depopulate Fraunce; that finallie hee slewe giauntes, and appalled the hartes of sterne and warlike menne. This redowted conqueror, of so manifolde exploits, is reported to have ben sodainle retrayted from his jornay with domesticall contention, while hee minded to invade Rome, and consequentlie to have extinguished his tratorus nephew, Mordred, who usurped the regall power in his absence, in which conflict hee himselfe received a fatall stroke and balefull wounde, whereof hee died.

And he disposes of the claims of the monks of Glastonbury with equal scorn:

Not manie years since in the abbey of Glastonburie was extructed for Arthur a magnificent sepulchre, that the posteritee might gather how worthie he was of all monuments, whearas in the dayse of Arthure this abbaye was not builded.

The immediate effect of these passages was to pre-cipitate a storm. Long before, Polydore had aroused suspicion. Andreas, secretary to the King and later his biographer, had asked Wolsey to warn his royal master against the foreigner. Later, as we shall see, Bale called upon Leland to show forth the treachery of this Italian Catholic. His attack on Geoffrey was esteemed mad-ness. Stories were circulated about his manipulation of evidence. Books were written against him, and long after, poets attacked him as a traitor to his adopted country. What were the reasons for this battle of the books?

II

With the accession of Henry VII the prophecies of Cadwallader, last of the Briton kings, were fulfilled and the realm returned to its rightful and ancient pos-sessors. Furthermore, patriotic Englishmen were quick to see that the new dynasty, marking the end of the Lancastrian-Yorkist feud, was far more significant than a mere change of monarchs. There emerged, as we shall see, two themes. One, the tragic story of Lancaster and York, ending in the union of England, was the theme of Hall's *Chronicle* and of Shakespeare's historical plays. The other, the return to power after many centuries of the ancient Britons, was the theme of Leland and other chroniclers, of Warner and Drayton who combined chronicle with epic, and of Spenser's *Faerie Queene*. These facts, once they are grasped, throw a flood of light upon the interpretation of a considerable portion of distinguished Elizabethan literature, and they illustrate the birth, as an accompaniment of the new national consciousness which was the outstanding achievement of the Tudors, of a striking form of historical primitivism.

Both these themes are found in solution in Hall's *Chronicle*. He writes " the history of Lancaster and York and the Union of England." The titles of his chapters or books prove the essentially dramatic conception of his story. After an introduction giving the story of the division between the two houses, he presents his subject according to the reigns, but with titles of great significance. He treats " the unquiet tyme of kyng Henry the Fowerth; the victorious actes of kyng Henry the v; the troubleous season of kyng Henry the vi; the prosperous reigne of kyng Edward the iiij; the pitifull life of kyng Edward the v; the tragicall doynges of kyng Richard the iij; the politike gouvernaunce of kyng Henry the vij; the triumphant reigne of king Henry the viij." Mr. C. L. Kingsford has recently pointed out that his chronicle was intended deliberately to be a glorification of the House of Tudor; that his version of the material was imbedded firmly in the opinion of the time and exerted profound influence not only upon Holinshed, the *Mirrour for Magistrates*, and Daniel's *Civil Wars* but also " culminated in the conception of dramatic unity which underlies the cycle of Shakespeare's Histories." This interpretation is convincing. Shakespeare's histories cover almost precisely the period covered by Hall. His plays might have used as subtitles some of the very words chosen by Hall to express his conception of the reigns he passed in review. Mingled with Shakespeare's treatment of the greatness of England's story is the constant warning of the dangers that spring from internal dissension. United, England is invincible. With the accession of the Tudors the way was open for this impregnable union that supplies an undercurrent of passionate nationalism throughout the plays. It is clearly apparent, then, that the interpretation of the significance of the accession of the Tudors given by Hall so appealed to other historians, poets, and dramatists as to become a powerful element in the formation of Elizabethan thought.

But we may also cite Hall to illustrate the other phase of our subject. In speaking of the accession of Henry Tudor he says:

> It was by a heavenly voyce reveled to Cadwalader last kyng of Brytons that his stocke and progeny should reigne in this land and beare domynion agayn: Whereupon most men were persuaded in their awne opinion that by this heavenly voice he [i. e. Hy vii] was provided and ordeined long before to enjoye and obteine this kyngdome, whiche thing kyng Henry the vi did also shewe before.

And we find in Hall, as in many other places, the explanation of the significance attached to the meaning of the first born son of the new monarch:

> Shortly after that to Wynchestre, where quene Elizabeth his wyfe was delivered of a fayre prynce named Arthur at his

baptyme. Of which name Englyshmen no more rejoysed then outwarde nacions and foreyne prynces trymbled and quaked, so much was that name to all nacions terrible and formidable.

Now both these ideas: that by the accession of Henry the ancient Britons were restored to their rights, and that Henry recognized this fact and its political value by giving to his first born the historic name of Arthur are met constantly in the literature of the sixteenth century. Coupled with it, we find emphasis upon the descent of the Britons from Troy and the superiority of the Britons in courage and manners to their Saxon conquerors. It is because Polydore denounced these claims as legendary that his book inspired controversy.

Polydore followed Gildas, who was Roman in sympathy, hated Celtic names, looked upon the Romans as powerful protectors, regarded the Britons as slaves eager to rebel when chance offered. So Polydore quotes not once but several times Gildas' statements concerning the cowardice of the Britons. He is impatient with that form of historical primitivism which seeks to exalt the supposed noble origin of the nation. "That book," he remarks contemptuously of Geoffrey's work, pretends that Brutus, son of Silvius, "begotten of Askanius the sonne of Aeneas," had been sent by Diana to Britain where he slew giants and founded the new nation. Not Livy nor Dionysius nor any other "did ever once make mention of this Brutus." Nevertheless, misguided patriots extol the ancient Britons above the

Romans and Macedonians; Roland is nothing to Arthur, who is exalted to the heavens. In the same spirit Erasmus mocked at historical primitivism, in his *Praise of Folly*. As it is with individuals, he says, so it is with nations. British, Scotch, French, Italians, all regard themselves as the only people on earth who are not absolute barbarians. Citizens of Rome are ravished with dreams of Rome's ancient greatness; the Venetians derive exquisite pleasure from a belief in their noble origin; the degenerate Greeks are no better—as if the birth of letters was in any respect due to them.

To Leland, on the other hand, such opinions were blasphemy, and it is not without significance that his translator, Richard Robinson, in 1582, added points of his own. Robinson's translation is dedicated to Lord Grey, of Wilton, Spenser's patron; to Sir Henry Sidney, father of another of his patrons, to Thomas Smith and the Society of Archers in London " yearely celebrating the renowmed memorie of the Magnificent Prince Arthure." Here, be it noted, we find the term " Prince " applied to Arthur, as Spenser used it, and the adjective "magnificent," eight years before the appearance of Spenser's poem on Arthur as Prince and as the embodiment of magnificence as chief of all the virtues. Robinson's dedicatory letter is shot through with the historical primitivism which Polydore and Erasmus derided:

The Hebrewes with greate and not indeserved titles extolled their Iudas Maccabeus. Homer the glory of all Greeke Poets left Hector and Achilles most commendable unto the worlde.

Neyther by lesse diligence did the Grecians adorne with praise Alexander the most mightie conquerour. And the Romanes advanced the noble actes of their Caesar to the Skyes not enough. The Burgonians profoundly praised Godfrey of Bulloyn (for his noble valiancy) as the scourge of the Sarazens in his dayes. And as every one of those are commended with due desert: so in like manner there were never Brittaines wanting of excellent learning and exquisite knowledge to leave with carefull diligence and credible commendation, the progenie, life, prowesse, prosperitie, and triumphant victories of our said auncient Arthure worthely published unto the worlde.

He refers to the significance of the name of Henry Tudor's first born son in a passage also significant for its praise of Leland, who was, he says, protected by Henry VIII as the defender of Arthur against the " cankered currish kinde of caveling carpers ":

By cause his elder brother being named Arthure, he him selfe a most christian King for all heroicall vertues commendable, the rather seemed to favour and further the advancement of the fame of his most renoumed auncester this same our ancient Arthure and the knightly traine of his rounde table.

And he quotes, with a translation, the dedicatory verses *ad candidos lectores* which give credit to Leland for glorifying Arthur against the evil sayings of Polydore:

Many yeeres surely Arthure hidden lay,
Of Brittons, the Glory, Light & Honor true:
Cheerely hath Leyland driven darke shadowes away,
And yeelds the world bright shining Sun to view.
Of Learned Readers, reioyce yee studious Crew,
He sincere did his Duetie bounden fulfill:
Farre hence flee those their spyte which spew,
Least their Intestines burst with their owne ill.

After stating his purpose to defend Arthur against the strictures of Polydore, Leland proceeds to give a more or less detailed biography. He has a formidable list of authorities, classical and British, but he is no match for Polydore in their use. He makes a palpable hit against "the adversary" in the suggestion that Polydore finds nothing credible which smelleth not of Tullie or Livy. He acknowledges that both obscure and absurd reports have crept into the history of Arthur, and these lead the curious to find fault. But surely there is no reason for holding that all is false; let us cast off old wives tales and superfluous fables and preserve what things are true, " for that whiche nowe a long time is embraced of Learned men with greate consent ought not in what soever moment of time barcking against it, together with faith or credite thereof, to be quite taken away." Of the deeds of Arthur against the Romans he will say nothing, but he accepts the Trojan origin of the Britons, accepts William of Malmesbury's account of the burial at Glastonbury, writes of Arthur's knights and of the Round Table, and then proceeds to give a list of testimonies gained from antiquities and from many writers, including Hector Boece who being a Scot hated the Britons, and " Polidorus the Italian." The account of the burial is given at great length and with an impressive list of authorities. The seventeenth chapter contains his most severe criticism of his rival, whose case, he rightly sees, turns chiefly on the credence to be given to Gildas, and he counters Gildas' strictures on British cowardice by citing many testimonies to their fame. The nationalist bias is most evident. As to Polydore's objection that the Roman writers say nothing of Arthur he rejoins: "If no thing be true but that which appeareth by truth of Romane writers, it should go evill to passe with the history of the whole worlde. The infinite force of thinges worthie of memory and of noble effect consisteth rather of eye witnesses at home resident and inhabiting then of the uncertaine relation made by forraine writers." The Romans took care of their own fame, but "the enterprises & actes of other Nations they dyd even so obscure and debase that almost they made them none at all." He seems to have the romances in mind in his statement that many impossible legends have become attached to the Arthurian story, but he makes a keen rejoinder by reminding us that the same is true of other great historical personages: Charlemagne, Roland, Godfrey, and the like; it is no reason against historicity to allege vain fables that attach to the great men of all nations. So also, one must guard against limitations or prejudices of the historians. Thus Bede, "though a good man and a learned, did not onely slenderly esteeme of the glory of Brittaines name, but also despysed or neglected it. For, there was some what adoe betwene them and the Saxons concerning the rule over Brittaine." He closes with a promise to set forth other matters concerning the greatness of Arthur and his people, "and at lengthe (those same most thicke

mistie cloudes in deede of ignorance being shaken off,
& utterly dashed aside) the light of Brittish Antiquitie
with displayed beames farre and wide shall shine forth."

Finally, the verses " Arturius Redivivus " at the end
of the book interpret the prophecy of Arthur's return
as fulfilled in Henry VIII.

This whole controversy about Polydore, therefore, is
illustrative of several matters of interest. It shows a
considerable contemporary interest in the Tudors as
inheritors of the old British supremacy, their accession
being the fulfillment of the old prophecies, and, naturally, a disposition to praise the ancient British virtues
as against the Saxons. There is evidence, as we have
seen, that the Tudors from the first made somewhat of
these matters as further justification of their claims.
Bacon reflects it in his history of Henry VII. He states
that the king's first son was named Arthur, " in honour
of the British race, of which himself was . . . according to the name of that ancient worthy King of the
Britons; in whose acts there is truth enough to make
him famous, besides that which is fabulous." And in
his account of the marriage of Prince Arthur, Bacon
writes:

In all the devices and conceits of the triumphs of this marriage, there was a great deal of astronomy. The lady being
resembled to Hesperus, and the Prince to Arcturus; and the
old King Alphonsus (that was the greatest astronomer of
Kings and was ancestor to the lady) was brought in to be the
fortune-teller of this match. And whosoever had those toys in
compiling, they were not altogether pedantical.

There is also, of course, the fact that much of the antagonism to Polydore sprang from the fact that he had no regard for the rising tide of national spirit. Welsh sympathisers naturally hailed with joy the accession of Henry Tudor. But the Scots were equally sensitive to racial superiority. We have already seen how James refused to give Polydore information that he wanted, on the ground that a foreigner could not do justice to Scottish virtues. Hector Boece was thoroughly nationalistic. His history celebrates the distinction of his countrymen and the cowardice and treachery of the Britons. He is as bitter against Arthur as Polydore himself, though for a quite different reason. The British were the first, he says, to celebrate Christmas in York with disgraceful orgies. Arthur's death was a just punishment for his failure to recognize Mordred as his successor. So late as the time of Holinshed we find references to this historical primitivism:

Of this Arthur manie things are written beyond credit, for that there is no ancient author of authoritie that confirmeth the same; but surelie as may be thought he was some woorthie man, and by all likelihood a great enimie to the Saxons, by reason whereof the Welshmen which are the verie Britains in deed have him in famous remembrance.

And Shakespeare, in *Henry the Fifth*, not only represents the peculiar racial characteristics of the various portions of English citizenry but introduces the political significance of the Tudor descent by making Fluellen boast of the Welsh descent of Henry, obviously a com-

pliment to those who rejoiced in the racial origin of
Queen Elizabeth.

Yet it would be a great mistake to look upon the
whole matter as nothing more than tribal or racial
jealousy. It was based on the most passionate love for
England and the hope in England's destiny now that the
long wars of the Roses were at an end, and it was based
on a new interest in the art and province of history.
Leland wrote to Henry VIII that he presented " a table
or map of your world and empery of England." He
studied faithfully all the chronicles, and desired to
arrive at the truth through travel to the places of historic interest and consulting the documents to be found
there. He studied, according to Bale, the British, Saxon,
and Welsh languages. Bale tells us that he saw in
Leland's study many works orderly digested, ready for
publication. Leland sought for permission to see the
books in various abbeys and monasteries. His *Itinerary*,
while primarily a record of monuments, contains many
notes about books that he consulted, or planned to consult. Bale argued that chronicles and old manuscripts
should be printed, for " the greate want of them hath
caused our latter chronicles, specyally Johan Hardynge,
Wyllyam Caxton, Robert Fabiane, and now last of all
Polydore Vergill so depely to erre as they have done in
so manye poyntes . . . To sende them fourth abroad
amonge men, for that purpose (I thynke) God hath in
thys age geven the noble art of prentynge."

This battle of the books, therefore, is of interest for

its contribution to our study of sixteenth century historiography. It is based partly on two conceptions of the proper use of sources and authorities. Polydore's method was that of the historical sceptic only in form, not substance. He said, "I do not believe," or "it is impossible," but the basis for the judgment, after all, was merely personal opinion, no matter how just that judgment, in certain cases, proved to be. His opponents, Leland, Churchyard, and the school of antiquaries to whom we owe so much, based their material on actual visits to places and the study of legends and history in what seemed to them to be a study of original sources. Leland, like William of Malmesbury so many years before him, actually went to Glastonbury in order to learn what he could. There was no British Museum in those days, filled with documents. And Leland, and his contemporaries and followers, saw rightly that merely clubbing authorities is not scholarship. The zeal of the tribal patriot became the passion for research. Camden, greatest of his school, speaks eloquently in defence of the study of antiquities as a means for acquiring a sense of historical truth. In his Preface to the Reader he refers to those who wholly condemn such studies as a "backlooking curiosity"; his own purpose is to be of service "to well bread and well-meaning men which tender the glory of their native Country"; and he continues:

In the studies of Antiquity (which is alwaies accompanied with dignity, and hath a certaine resemblance with eternity)

there is a sweet food of the minde well befitting such as are
of honest and noble disposition. If any there be which are
desirous to be strangers in their owne soile, and forrainers in
their owne City, they may so continue and therein flatter themselves. For such like I have not written these lines, nor taken
these paines.

And a modern scholar who has himself made notable
contributions to antiquarian research, the Dean of Wells,
remarks:

> The task is laborious, but it has a peculiar fascination for
> those who interest themselves in the processes of the medieval
> mind, who are not content on the one hand to accept traditions
> as probably true because they were told and believed, or on the
> other hand to dismiss them at once as what are called monkish
> tales. History is not merely a record of facts: it has to do with
> causes and effects, with the development of ideas and the
> growth of institutions. The first emergence of a tradition, its
> enrichment by successive generations, its localisation in par-
> ticular spots—all this concerns the historian, who cannot afford
> to neglect the gradual growth of any kind of belief. Con-
> sidered from this point of view the *residuum* of fact which may
> be shewn to underlie a local tradition is less important than the
> discovery of the stages through which the tradition has passed,
> and the causes which appear to have determined its develop-
> ment.

Enough has been said, I think, to show that whatever
the original political significance of the Arthurian legend
may have been, the story took on new life with the
accession of the Tudors and with the quarrel about
Polydore Vergil's history. It is a curious repetition.
Appearing in Layamon and Geoffrey as history mixed

with fable, it stimulated enormously the development of a courtly literature in the cycles of romance. Revived in the early part of the sixteenth century, it became identified with Tudor politics, embodied an historical primitivism that accompanied the growth of the new national spirit, stimulated the study and writing of history, and then, once more, became the inspiration of a new literary cycle.

III

It is true that Polydore was not the first to look with suspicion upon British nationalist claims. For example, the author of the St. Alban's Chronicle of 1440 had maintained that the story of the Trojan origin of the Britons was poetical rather than historical. True nobility, he said, is by deeds, not by descent. " It is a vaine opinion and ridiculous to challenge noble blood and yet to want a probable ground of the challenge: for it is manhood onely that enobleth a nation. . . Let this suffice, that the Britaines from the beginning of their nobilitie have been courageous and valiant in fight, that they have subdued their enemies on every side, and that they utterly refused the yoke of servitude." Here we have Polydore's suspicion of legendary origins, but without his personal animus against the Britons, an animus, carried, as we have seen, against Arthur as the chief British hero.

The controversy begun by Polydore and Leland may be traced throughout the historical writings of the Tudor period. We may omit merely racial claims such as those set up by Arthur Kelton in his " Chronycle with a Genealogye declarying that the Brittons and Welshmen are lineallye dyscended from Brute " (1547), and which distinguished between the Romans, led by "Polidorus" and "us Welshmen," or the *Historiae Brytannicae Defensio* of Price (1573). Camden is more important, both for his contribution to the development of English historiography and for his position with reference to British primitivism.

In his preface "to the Reader" of the *Britannia* Camden disavows prejudice:

> I have done dishonour to no nation, have descanted upon no mans name, I have impaired no mans reputation, I have impeached no mans credit, no not Geffray of Monmouth whose history (which I would gladly support) is heald suspected amongst the judicious. Neither have I assumed upon my selfe any perswasion of knowledge, but onely that I have beene desirous to know much.

His method unites antiquarianism and the historical theory of Polydore. He gives some account of the geographical situation of Britain, discusses the origins, gives information concerning the Druids, and treats the manners and customs of the Britons. One feels that he passes with relief to the more certain records about Roman Britain, drawn, as he says, " not out of feined fables, which were vanitie to recite, and meere folly to beleeve, but out of the incorrupt and ancient moniments." Arthur plays a somewhat minor part in his history; he has no special leaning to the Britons; but there is much in his account that bears, however impersonally, upon the subject of historical primitivism.

After criticising the theory of Trojan origin, Camden speaks of similar claims made by the French, who derive, some hold, from Francio a Trojan, son of Priam, and continues:

> Hence they collect, that when our country-men heard once how the French-men their neighbours drew their line from the Trojans, they thought it a foule dishonour, that those should outgoe them in nobilitie of Stocke, whom they matched every way in manhood and proesse. Therfore, that Geffrey ap Arthur of Monmouth foure hundred yeares agoe, was the first, as they thinke, that to gratifie our Britains produced unto them this Brutus, descended from the gods, by birth also a Trojan, to be the author of the British nation.

Similar historical primitivism Camden finds in other nations. For example, the Scots derive, it is held, from Scota, the " Aegyptian Pharaoh's daughter"; the Irish, Danes, Goths, and Saxons have similar legends. The French have repudiated their Francio, though one Turnebus maintains that they still " stand highly upon their descent from the Trojans, they doe it in emulation of the Romans, whom they seeing to beare themselves proud of that Pedegree and noble stocke, would needs take unto themselves also the like reputation." But on the whole, such fanciful matters are in the discard by other peoples and he says that many are asking why we should cling to the old legends, " as if there had not

lived many valorous men before Agamemnon." The
" grave Senate of great Clerks "—Boccace, Vives, Polydore, Buchanan, Bodin, deny that there ever was a
Brutus. The Abbot of St Albans, he holds, was right
in denying that there was ever such son of Ascanius:

wherefore, it is . . . a vaine piece of worke (says John), and
ridiculous enough to challenge noble blood and yet to want a
probable ground of the challenge.

Others are cited who accuse Geoffrey of extolling the
Britons far above the valorous Macedonians and
Romans. It is highly significant, however, that he
summarizes as follows:

For mine owne part, let Brutus be taken for the father and
founder of the British nation: I will not be of a contrarie minde
. . . I wot full well, that Nations in old time for their originall
had recourse unto Hercules, and in later ages to the Trojans.
Let Antiquity heerein be pardoned, if by entermingling falsi-
ties and truthes, humane matters and divine together, it make
the first beginnings of nations and cities more noble, sacred,
and of greater maiestie.

With Speed (1611) the wheel has come full circle.
His account of the early Britons is based on Caesar and
other classical authorities. The Britons led mean lives,
they had little learning, but the historian speaks of the
" glory of this ancient and warlike nation " in terms
quite different from those employed by Polydore. The
Romans themselves, he says, " bring their name and
originall from Romulus, a bastard by birth, nourished
by a beast, educated among a sort of rusticke shep-

heards, and, growne to the ripeness of his owne affections, he became ringleader of a damned crue that lived by robberies and without lawes." He rejects Geoffrey as an authority, gives a brief account of Arthur's twelve battles, says he will omit the usual accounts of his "magnificence," on which one may consult "Monmouth the Writer, Newbery the Resister, and Leiland the Maintainer." He agrees with Malmesbury that Arthur was a prince better praised for his real deeds than "by fables scandalized with poeticall fictions and hyperbolicall falshoods." For adding so many toys and tales to the record, Geoffrey "is now ranged among those writers whom the Roman Church hath censured to be forbidden." Yet Speed accepts the record of the burial at Glastonbury; the prophecy of Cadwallader's return he rejects, and does not connect it with Henry VII. Some faint suggestion of the quarrel remains in his reference to John Lewis, "the Reformer of the British history," who despite his defence of Geoffrey and his complaints against Camden "for blowing away sixty of the Britaine Kings with one blast," yet cannot fill the gap. It is Camden's position which he adopts: "Let us give leave to Antiquity, who sometimes mingles falsehoods with truths, to make the beginnings of Policies seem more honourable."

Thus the racial enthusiasm which burst forth when Henry Tudor entered Milford Haven on the Welsh coast and advanced under the red-dragon standard of Cadwallader to claim the long vacant British throne finds both literary and political significance. The battle of the books had many important results. It sharpened the perception of writers to the nature of historical evidence. It stimulated enormously the growth of the antiquarian spirit, and thus made a notable contribution to the progress of learning. It contributed to the rising tide of nationalism, illustrating the development from a mere device of political expediency—the claim of the Tudors to Arthur's seat — to a historical primitivism. Some of these aspects of the battle are even more clearly registered in the imaginative literature of the time than in the work of the chroniclers and historians, and to these we now turn.

The transition from history to romance may be traced in the evolution of the *Mirrour for Magistrates*. The original plan of the work had been to reprint Lydgate with a continuation to the middle of the sixteenth century. Ferrers expressed surprise that the Britons, Danes, Saxons and English had been omitted. With the edition of 1574 we are introduced to the tragedies of British kings " from the coming of Brute," and the editor, John Higgins, wrote in his Preface of the importance of the new material:

I have seen no auncient antiquities in written hand but two: one was Galfridus of Monmouth, which I lost be misfortune; the other, an old chronicle in a kind of English verse, beginning at Brute and ending at the death of Humfrey, Duke of Gloucester; in the which, and divers other good chronicles, I finde many things not mentioned in that great tome engrossed of late by Maister Grafton, and that, where he is most barraine and wantes matter.

By 1610 the imitation or continuation of Lydgate had so developed as to be styled "A true chronicle history of the untimely falles of such unfortunate Princes and men of note, as have happened since the first entrance of Brute." Professor Cunliffe has spoken of the influence of the *Mirrour* as derived "through the interest it aroused in the national history," and refers to Daniel, Drayton, and Warner, as well as to the chronicle plays. But we may also note its influence on such allegorical plays as *Gorboduc* and *The Misfortunes of Arthur,* with their clear reference to Tudor affairs, and upon Spenser, whose material, drawn from the chronicles, as Miss Harper has shown, yet has the moral tone of the *Mirrour* and introduces the same personages. But the *Mirrour* does not contain, save by implication, the racial and national elements characteristic of the quarrel begun by Polydore. Its importance is rather in its proof of continued interest in the personages of Geoffrey's story and of the vitality of this story despite the attacks made upon it.

IV

The battle of the books passes to the bards. Druid-like they sang the fulfillment of Merlin's prophecies—Warner, Churchyard, Drayton. In Spenser, past, present, and future were united. Drawing inspiration from "Briton moniments", confirming in Elizabeth Tudor the return of Arthur's line, moralizing chivalry as a model for the new age, visioning the expansion of Britain to world empire like Arthur's—the *Faerie Queene* is intimately connected with the matter of the Battle in spirit as well as content. These things we shall see better when the poem is related to the group to which it belongs, and in a study of this relation we shall find reason both for the great popularity of the poem in its own time and, indirectly, a guide to the "continued allegory" which Spenser says that it contains.

And first, Churchyard. *The Worthines of Wales* (1587) is dedicated to Queen Elizabeth; his purpose is "to set foorth a worke in the honour of Wales, where your highnes auncestors tooke name." He cites David Powell's invective against Polidore and his accomplices for their "lying tongues, envyous detraction, malicious slanders, reproachfull and venomous language, wilfull ignorance, dogged crime, and canckered mindes, for that thei spake unreverently of Arthur." In the poem itself, he speaks of the singers of the origins of nations. Homer gave praise to the Greeks as against the Trojans, and Livy did the same for his countrymen in later days. So Polydore is to be accounted a Roman, his purpose being, as in all national panegyrists, "to blurre strange soyles" in order to celebrate the prowess of his countrymen. So Polydore writes not only with bias against the enemies of his people but also without full knowledge. He knew nothing of Wales, saw little of Britain, and loved it not. To such a man, tales of national origins of the Britons are of no account, but

> Though we count but Robin Hood a jest,
> And old wives tales, as talting toyes appeare:
> Yet Arthurs raigne the world cannot denye,
> Such proofe there is, the troth therof to trye,
> That who so speakes against so grave a thing
> Shall blush to blot the fame of such a King.

This historical primitivism which praises the singers of
the founders of nations, recognizes that the national
panegyrist praises his own countrymen at the expense
of rivals, and calls for bards to do justice to the origins
of Britain, is strong in Churchyard, who ranges Polydore, as his predecessors had done, with the Romans.
He proceeds to plead for the recognition of Carleon as
the seat of the ancient British virtue:

> King Arthurs raigne (though true it weare)
> Is now of small account:
> The fame of Troy is knowne each where,
> And to the skyes doth mount:
> Both Athens, Theabes, and Carthage too
> We hold of great renowne:
> What then I pray you shall we doe
> To poore Carleon Towne.
> King Arthur sure was crowned there;
> It was his royall seate.

And he concludes this praise with a direct appeal to
Elizabeth:

> Would God the brute thereof were knowne,
> In countrey, courte, and towne:
> And she that sits in reagall Throne
> With sceptre, sword, and crowne,

(Who came from Arthurs race and lyne)
　Would marke these matters throwe:
And shewe thereon her gracious eyne,
　To help Carleon now.

In *Albions England*, Warner extended the background uniting Albion with classical story. As a result the first two books are required to bring us down to the coming of Brute. The third book begins the chronicle of British kings, and in the fourth book the Saxons are represented as tyrants. The comment he makes on Cadwallader, last of the British kings, in Book III, and the reference to the prophecy as being fulfilled by the accession of Henry Tudor, in Book VII, will serve to show the provenience of his work:

Cadwallader, in leaving thus
　His native shore, he fixt
His eyes from whence his bodie should,
　And with his sighes he mixt
His royal teares, which giving place,
　He speaketh thus betwixt . . .

So, Brutaine, thou of nation and
　Of name indurest change,
Now balking us whome thou hast bread,
　And brooking people strange.

Yet (if I shoot not past mine aime)
　A world of time for me,
Part of our blood, in highest pompe,
　Shall Englands glorie be:
And chieflie, when unto a first
　Succeeds a second she.

(Book III, c. 19)

So not with Yorke and Lancaster
    Doth wonted envie raigne,
Nor can Aeneas off-spring now
    Of orphansie complaine.

But that Cadwallader's fore-doomes
    In Tuders should effect
Was unexpected, save that God
    Doth destinies direct.

(Book VII, c. 34)

Both in time of composition and of publication,
Polyolbion belongs to the Stuarts and not to the Tudors.
In the text, and in Selden's notes, the accession of
James, descendant of Welsh stock through the escape
of Fleance, is seen, as in *Macbeth*, as the fulfillment of
ancient prophecy. The work illustrates the passionate
regret of the antiquarians for Time's destruction of
ancient monuments, and is designed in part to stimulate
popular interest in antiquities. Thus Drayton is of the
line of Leland, of Camden, and of Spenser. Moreover,
Polyolbion grew out of Drayton's long interest in the
rhymed chronicle as a form of history. He had collaborated in the writing of many historical plays. He
had dealt in earlier poems with stories of post-Norman
times, some of his subjects being identical with those
used by writers of the historical plays. Just as Shakespeare turned at length from Lancastrian and Yorkist
themes to tragic legends of British history such as *Lear*
and *Macbeth*, so Drayton makes of *Polyolbion* not so
much an itinerary as a repository of British legend. The
chorographical description is there, certainly, as in

Leland and Camden, but it seems less vital. Its author was no peripatetic, and much of his information about persons and places appears to have been got up by industrious and select reading; it is the frame-work, and may be disregarded by those who are seeking for what gives to the poem whatever vitality it possesses.

Already in the *Heroical Epistles* Drayton had referred to the matters which we are now considering. In the letter of Queen Katherine to Owen Tudor, the lady speaks of the greatness of Wales. The English, she says, boast of their " conquest of your land," but they won their victories hardly. And in Owen's reply we learn that he went from Wales to England not because of Henry's fame or for any other reason:

> But by th' eternall Destinies consent
> Whose uncomprised wisedomes did foresee
> That you in marriage should be linck'd to mee.
> By our great Merlin was it not fore-told
> (Amongst his holy prophesies enrold)
> When first he did of Tudors name devine,
> That Kings and Queens should follow in our line?

This passage brings us into the presence of the prophecies of Merlin, so large an element in *Polyolbion*. For while Drayton's territory is all the English scene and English history, he wrote most of Wales and of the ancient Britons. Moreover, he invents, or adapts, a mythology suitable to his purpose. There are contests of Druid bards; rivers personified as goddesses are given realms and teach their subjects the meaning of ancient history. There is a contest between Britons and the English, presided over by Sabrine, who is described in terms reminding us of the goddess Natura in Spenser's *Mutabilitie*. And these various divinities in Drayton's poem are accompanied by the learned John Selden, himself an authority in ancient law, like the grave Palmer who instructs Spenser's Guyon, and in the "illustrations" which Selden gives by way of annotation we see clearly enough the true intent of Drayton's poem.

Examples of this co-ordination of text and illustration are everywhere found. For instance, clear application of Merlin's prophecies to the accession of Henry Tudor is found in Song II:

> As brought into her mind the Eagle's prophecies;
> Of that so dreadful plague, which all great Britain swept,
> From that which highest flew, to that which lowest crept,
> Before the Saxon thence the Briton should expel,
> And all that there upon successively befel.
> How then the bloody Dane subdu'd the Saxon race;
> And, next, the Norman took possession of the place:
> Those ages once expired, the fates to bring about,
> The British line restored, the Norman lineage out.
> Then, those prodigious signs to ponder she began, . . .

On which compare Selden's gloss:

This Eagle (whose prophecies among the Britons, with the later of Merlin, have been of no less respect than those of Bacis were to the Greeks, or the Sybillines to the Romans) foretold of a reverting of the crown, after the Britons, Saxons, and Normans, to the first again, which in Henry the Seventh, grandchild to Owen Tyddour, hath been observed as fulfilled (Twin, in Albionic. 2). This in particular is peremptorily affirmed by the count Palatine of Basingstoke. Et aperte dixit, tempus aliquando fore, ut Britannium imperium denuo sit ad veteres Britannos post Saxonas & Normannos rediturum, are the words of this eagle.

Selden goes on to say that it is not the prophecy of an eagle but that through

an angelical voice, almost seven hundred years after Christ, given to Cadwallader (whom some call Cedwalla) that restitution of the crown to the Britons is promised.

In the notes to the third song there is much lore of Cheddar, the Mendips, and Glastonbury, and Selden refers to Arthur's return, with a quotation of Lydgate's lines, " He is a king," etc.

Song IV is taken up with a great contest between England and Wales. The argument:

> England and Wales strive, in this song;
> To whether Lundy doth belong:
> When either's nymphs, to clear the doubt,
> By music mean to try it out.
> Of mighty Neptune leave they ask:
> Each one betakes her to her task.
> The Britons, with the harp and crowd:
> The English, both with still and loud.
> The Britons chant king Arthur's glory;
> The English sing their Saxon's story.
> The hills of Wales their weapon's take,
> And are an uproar like to make,
> To keep the English part in awe.

Here we have treated imaginatively the subject of the great Quarrel. The contest is decided by Sabrine. Drayton achieves considerable imaginative flights in his description of the scene. The goddess, in an imperial chair, clad in a watchet weed, with coral fringed, her path strewn with pearl, sits like some great learned judge, before a mighty rout, with constant brow and firm and settled thought; the people crowd near to learn the decision. It is this scene, in its setting and its persons, that reminds us of the trial of Mutability before the assembly of the gods:

> My near and loved nymphs, good hap ye both betide:
> Well Britons have ye sung; your English, well reply'd:
> Which to succeeding times shall memorize you stories
> To either country's praise, as both your endless glories.
> And from your list'ning ears, sith vain it were to hold
> What all-appointing Heaven will plainly shall be told,
> Both gladly be you pleas'd: for thus the powers reveal,
> That when the Norman line in strength shall lastly fail
> (Fate limiting the time) th' ancient Briton race
> Shall come again to sit upon the sovereign place.
> A branch sprung out of Brute, th' imperial top shall get,
> Which grafted in the stock of great Plantagenet,
> The stem shall strongly wax, as still the trunk doth wither:
> That power which bare it thence, again shall bring it thither
> By Tudor, with fair winds from Little Britain driven,
> To whom the goodly bay of Milford shall be given
> As thy wise prophets, Wales, foretold his wish'd arrive,
> And how Lewellin's line in him should doubly thrive.

This theme is returned to, in one form or another, throughout the poem. There is long and eloquent defense of the Britons by the River Wye near the end of Song VI. Here we find praise of the bards for their influence over soldiers; the Britons are greater than the Saxons; they are naturally infused with poetic rage, and they are praised for their poetry in terms that anticipate the revival of interest in the old poetry that was one characteristic of eighteenth-century romanticism. Drayton seems also to have Polydore in mind in the lines in which the goddess exclaims:

> Here then I cannot choose but bitterly exclaim
> Against those fools that all antiquity defame,
> Because they have found out, some credulous ages laid
> Slight fictions with the truth, whilst truth on rumour staid.

It is the rule, Drayton says, that when a thing has been found true, it may become mingled with a fiction that gives colour and interest; but at this

> our critics gird, whose judgments are so strict,
> And he the bravest man who most can contradict
> That which decrepit age (which forced is to lean
> Upon tradition) tells; esteeming it so mean,
> As they it quite reject, and for some trifling thing
> (Which time hath pinn'd to truth) they all away will fling,
> These men (for all the world) like our precisians be,
> Who for some cross or saint they in the window see
> Will pluck down all the church.

In Song V we also find the continuance of the British tradition to celebrate the union of Scotland with England through the accession of James, the theme, at least in part, of Shakespeare's *Macbeth*. Through the escape of Fleance, his reception by Gryffith ap Lhewelin, and the marriage of his daughter into the family from which the Stuarts sprang, the way was opened for the eventual union of Tudor, Stuart, and Plantagenet blood. Selden's notes explain the details, and are so nearly contemporary with *Macbeth* as to leave no doubt as to the way in which Shakespeare's tragedy was interpreted in the opening years of the seventeenth century.

With these matters we are not at present concerned. The theme of *Polyolbion*, for us, is the exaltation of the Britons as against the Saxons, the vindication of the legend against the attacks of Polydore and his school, and the celebration of the Tudor house in the same terms as those employed by Spenser. We even find, in Song VIII, re-affirmation of the Trojan descent:

> My Wales, then hold thine own, and let thy Britons stand
> Upon their right, to be the noblest of the land.
> Think how much better 'tis, for thee, and those of thine,
> From gods, and heroes old to draw your famous line,
> Than from the Scythian poor; whence they themselves derive,
> Whose multitudes did first you to the mountains drive.

Here is the latest stand of the British historical primitivism; Drayton is at one with Leland; it is the vindication of the Tudors as Britons. With it we may compare Selden's note:

> It pleases the Muse in this passage to speak of that original (the Saxons) as mean and unworthy of comparison with the Trojan British, drawn out of Jupiter's blood by Venus, Anchises, and Aeneas; I justify her phrase, for that the Scythian was indeed poor, yet voluntarily, not through want.

But he goes on to say that the Saxons were also worthy in descent, with learned references to prove his point. The whole passage and Selden's note on it thus indicates the change as we pass into the seventeenth century. The Drayton theme is pretty certainly early, and Tudor; the note is of the following century. Milton, interested in the origins of parliamentary government, looks upon the Britons as the barbarians and exalts their conquerors.

We may note, finally, a singular recurrence of the issues of the Battle in Robert Chester's *Love's Martyr* (1601). This poem has attracted attention beyond its merits because of its inclusion, in a poetical miscellany which follows Chester's work, of "The Phoenix and the Turtle" ascribed to Shakespeare, and because of Grosart's unfortunate assumption that the allegory of the poem refers to the love of Elizabeth for Essex. For our purpose, its importance consists in the story of the life and death of King Arthur which is interpolated, somewhat awkwardly, into the midst of the poem. This story, with the Preface which introduces it, revives the old quarrel. After the account of the journey to the various British cities, which suggests some of the topographical surveys of which the Elizabethan antiquaries were so fond, we are told about Windsor, built by Arviragus and finished by Arthur,

> Of whose rare deedes our Chronicles do ring
> And poets in their verse his praise do sing
> For his Round-table and his war-like Fights,
> Whose valiantness the coward Mind affrights.

Arthur, we are told, was a companion of the Order of the Garter, and at Windsor created 140 knights; he slew his Saxon foes, and is remembered as the personification of that spirit which makes England's foes to tremble. Into this setting is introduced the story of the birth, life, death, and burial of the great king, prefaced by an address to the reader in which Chester states that he had been intreated by some of his friends to insert such a story:

By reason that there yet remains in this doubtfull age of opinions, a controversie of that esteemed Prince of Brittaine, to write not according to ages oblivion, but directed onely by our late Historiographers of England, who no doubt have taken great paines in the searching foorth of the truth of that first Christian worthie: and wheras (I know not directed by what blindnes) there have bene some Writers (as I thinke enemies to truth) that in their erronious censures have thought no such man ever to be living. How fabulous that should seeme to be, I leave to the judgement of the best readers, who know for certaine, that that never dead Prince of memory, is more beholding to the French, the Romane, the Scot, the Italian, yea to the Greekes themselves, then to his own Country-men, who have fully and wholly set foorth his fame and liveli-hood: then how shameless is it for some of us, to let slip the truth of this Monarch?

It is noticeable that the chronicle itself deals with the topics treated by Leland, but that Chester used Robin-son's translation rather than the original. He draws upon the notes which Robinson added to his translation for the description of Arthur's shield, saying, like Robinson, that he translates from " a certaine French booke." Part of this description he puts into verse, following closely, however, Robinson's prose. Furthermore, at the end of his chronicle, Chester prints "the true Pedigree" of Arthur, all of it in verse; Robinson has it in his additional notes, with only four lines in meter, the rest prose. Finally, the Epitaph is copied from Robinson, not Leland, for Chester uses Robinson's Latin description of it, and Robinson's reprint of the text, which differs in several details from Leland's text. For these reasons, it seems probable that Chester got his material from Robinson several years before his final use of his work in *Love's Martyr*; it may very well be, as he says, the first work of a new British poet. But it is by no means unrelated to the main theme of *Love's Martyr*. Sir John Salusbury was descended from Henry VII, and it is in compliment to the Tudor ancestry of his patron and his interest in Welsh antiquities that Chester inserted this vindication of Arthur into a poem dealing, as Professor Brown has shown, with the life of his patron.

V

Thus far ample evidence has been given to prove that the matter of Britain was constantly in men's minds through the Tudor period, and that it was the subject not only of historiographers but of poets as well. There was no attempt to inject the legends of the great knights; Malory was read but was without literary influence. The effort was to prove Arthur's historicity, his greatness as a founder of the nation, and the fulfillment of the ancient prophecies with the accession of the Tudors. If we turn, now, to records in state papers, to masques and entertainments presented at court, and to certain dramas, we shall find further illustrations.

There are, of course, frequent references in the State Papers to the Order of the Garter, which was regarded by Henry VII as "the badge and first order of King Arthur." Henry VIII carried to the Field of Cloth of Gold pageantry suggestive of Arthur the world conqueror. In a description of the entertainment at the banqueting house in Calais, July 12, 1520, we learn that

The centre figure represented King Arthur in regal apparel, and at his feet a scroll, across which were three royal crowns, and beneath, eight verses in French to this effect: ' I am the famous King Arthur, come to behold you, valorous Princes: be welcome,' etc.   On the left hand was a man-at-arms in armour carrying a spear, and at his feet a scroll bearing the old arms of England, and beneath the motto—' Amicus fidelis est alter ego.'   Between this figure (i. e. of the man-at-arms) and King Arthur was the red dragon (King Henry's badge) bearing the banner or arms of England . . . Beneath the verses about King Arthur was a gilt shield, and two hands, in each of which was a drawn sword, and a scroll round them inscribed with the words ' Cui adhaero praeest' which induced much comment.

Even in the last days of Henry, it was still possible to compare him with Arthur. An entry dated 11 October, 1533, indicates the increasing foreign troubles and the decadence of the king's reputation among foreign observers:

It is also said great mortal war will be made against England, and all the King's supporters will be slain by the sword, ' but they will not brenne.' They intend to make war on Calais, and they have no doubt that Andrea Doria, if the Emperor give him men enough, will conquer England. All that know the King have great pity at his misordering, considering his great nobleness and fame, which is greater than that of any prince since King Arthur.

The letter of Eustace Chapuys, from London, to the Emperor represents a hostile attitude, but gives testimony again to Tudor claims for greatness based upon the conquests of Arthur. After a lengthy account of an interview with the Duke of Norfolk on the question of the King's conflict with the Pope with regard to the divorce of Katharine, we read:

After the above arguments (which I think were taken in good part) the Duke went on to say that some days ago he had had occasion to shew to the French ambassador a copy of the inscription on the tomb of King Arthur (I could not understand at the time to which of the Arthurs he alluded), which inscription he produced in a parchment roll out of his pouch and handed over to me, adding that he had caused it to be transcribed for my use. I looked at it, and saw only these words written in large letters Patricius Arcturus Britannie Gallie, Germanie, Dacie Imperator. My answer was that I was sorry to see that he was not entitled also Emperor of Asia, Imperator Asie, as he might have left the present King Henry for his successour in such vast dominions . . . If by shewing me the inscription the Duke meant that the present King Henry might be such a conqueror as Arthur, I could not help observing that the Assyrians, Persians, Macedonians, and

Romans had also made great conquests, and everyone knew what had become of their empire.

Other similar illustrations might be given. So late as 1595, Walter Quin, an Irishman who was asked by King James to reply to Spenser's characterization of Mary Stuart, wrote, in a treatise of poetry dedicated to James, a series of sonnets some of which were inscribed " Charles James Stewart claims Arthur's seat," and " Charles James Stewart, ceas letts I am Arthur." And it will be remembered that much was made, upon James's accession, of the fact that he fulfilled the ancient prophecies about the return of the British line.

The case with respect to Queen Elizabeth is not less clear. One of the pageants at her coronation represented her right to the throne by descent from Henry Tudor and the ending of the strife of Lancaster and York. A similar motif was used at the entertainment of the Queen at Norwich in 1578. For the Arthurian motif, however, the outstanding example among the Queen's Progresses was the pageant at Kenilworth in 1575. Like so many Elizabethan entertainments, the material is a combination of British legendary remains and classical myth. The work of Gascoigne and his collaborators was Arthurian in its setting: the porter, the gate, the six giant trumpeters, the lake, with the Lady " so conveyed that it seemed shee had gone upon the water," etc. After this, classical influence predominates in the Echo passage, the debate about the nymph Zabeta; the shepherd destroyed by love (Leicester);

the nymphs with Diana; the plea for Leicester by Gascoigne garbed as Sylvanus. But the Arthurian provenience is unquestionable. The interpretation placed upon the six giant trumpeters, we are told, was "that in the daies and reigne of King Arthure, men were of that stature; so that the Castle of Kenelworth should seeme still to be kept by Arthur's heires and servants." Of interest also are the verses by Ferrers, sometime Lord of Misrule. These came at the first of the pageant, being a part of the welcome by the Lady of the Lake:

Though haste say on, let sute obtain some stay,
    (Most peerles Prince, the honour of your kinde,)
While that in short my state I doe display,
    And yeelde you thanks for that which now I finde,
Who erst have wisht that death me hence had fet;
    If Gods not borne to die had ought death any det.

I am the Lady of this pleasant Lake,
    Who, since the time of great King Arthure's reigne,
That here with royal Court abode did make,
    Have led a lowring life in restless paine,
Till now, that this your third arrival here,
    Doth cause me come abroad, and bodly thus appeare.

For after him such stormes this Castle shooke,
    By swarming Saxons first who scourgde this land,
As foorth of this my Poole I neer durst looke.
    Though Kenelme King of Merce did take in hand
(As sorrowing to see it in deface)
    To reare these ruines up, and fortifie this place.

For straight by Danes and Normans all this Ile
    Was sore distrest, and conquered at last;

> Whose force this Castle felt, and I therewhile
>   Did hide my head; and though it straightway past
> Unto Lord Sentloe's hands, I stode at bay,
>   And never shewed myselfe, but still in keepe I lay.

So the Lady goes on to trace the history of the Castle during the long period from Arthur's death until the present:

> Tyl now the Gods doe seeme themselves t'allow
>   My comming foorth, which at this time reveale
> My number due, that your thrice comming here
>   Doth bode thrise happy hope, and voides the place
>   from feare.

> Wherefore I wil attend while you lodge here,
>   (Most peereles Queene) to Court to make resort;
> And as my love to Arthure dyd appeere,
>   So shal't to you in earnest and in sport.
> Pass on, Madame, you need no longer stand;
>   The Lake, the Lodge, the Lord, are yours for to
>   command.

In letters, in occasional verses, and in the masques are numerous evidences of the survival of this historical primitivism throughout the period. Henry VIII seemed to the Venetian secretary to be a reincarnation of St. George himself. The saint appeared in many a pageant, as well as in the mumming shows. It is noteworthy that several of the little illustrative couplets or stanzas introduced into the *Arte of English Poesie* refer to the Trojan origin of the nation, and to Queen Elizabeth as representative of the tradition:

Elizabeth regent of the great Brittaine Ile,
Honour of all regents and of Queenes . . .

which is immediately followed by reference to

The English Diana, the great Britton mayde.

In further compliment to the Queen, the author gives
as an example of Antonomasia a third allusion to " the
most great and famous mayden of all Brittayne " thus:

But in chaste stile, am borne as I weene
To blazon foorth the Brytton mayden Queene.

Peele's London pageants, as might be expected, often
refer to the supposed descent from Troy: the Lord
Mayor's pageant of 1585 expresses this idea, and in the
more elaborate *Descensus Astreae* (1591) we are told,
first, of the goddess descended from Jove, now to be
identified with Elizabeth,

Descended of the Trojan Brutus' line,
Offspring of that courageous conquering king,
Whose pure renown hath pierced the world's large ears,
In golden scrolls rolling about the heavens;
Celestial sacred Nymph, that tends her flock
With watchful eyes, and keeps this fount in peace, etc.

" Our fair Astraea " is shown with her shepherds,
repelling Superstition and Ignorance, and attended by
all the virtues and the muses. Similar references are
found in Peele's *Anglorum Feriae*, 1595 (written in
celebration of the Queen's accession to the throne),
which is an interesting illustration of the reviews of the
Queen's services in freeing England from foreign domi-

nation that regularly accompanied celebrations of her coronation. The true significance of this long poem is not in the chance references to British antiquity but in its review of the chief events of the reign as seen through Elizabethan eyes. It shares this distinction with other coronation day poems characteristic of the time; it is like *Elizabetha Triumphans* by James Ashe (1588) and Niccols's *England's Eliza*; and all the poems of the genre are to be compared with the *Faerie Queene*, which, after all, is to be regarded as a celebration of those qualities and deeds of Elizabeth which caused her poets to compare her to Arthur of Britain and to see in her reign a revival of the old golden age.

These grave matters, and their bearing on the proper interpretation of Spenser's allegory, I shall discuss in another place. Such references and allusions as are mentioned here, with many others which might be cited, suffice to show that the descent of the Britons from the Trojans, the linking of Arthur, Henry VIII, and Elizabeth as Britain's greatest monarchs, and the return under Elizabeth of the Golden Age, are all commonplaces of Elizabethan thought. Peele, in *The Honour of the Garter* (1593), lists the three monarchs in his vision of the worthies of the world:

> And Arthur, glory of the western world,
> And all his knights were in this royal train . . .

> A prince of famous memory I saw,
> Henry the Eight, that led a warlike band
> Of English earls, and lords, and lusty knights,
> That ware the garter sacred to Saint George. . . .

I saw a virgin queen, attired in white,
Leading with her a sort of goodly knights.

The considerable group of dramas dealing with events
in British history possesses, with one or two exceptions,
little importance for our inquiry. They testify to a con-
tinuing interest in the matter of the chronicles; they
depend on those portions of the *Mirrour for Magistrates*
which the editor of that work reports as wanting in the
work of Polidore and his school, and with the monarchs
who figure in Spenser's chronicle in the *Faerie Queene*.
Some of them celebrate the valor of the Britons, usually,
of course, in contrast with the Romans, not with the
Saxons. They avoid the romantic and supernatural
character of Arthurian legend, confine themselves to
what the authors seem to have regarded as authentic
history. A good example of their spirit is *Fuimus Troes:
The True Trojans*, by Dr. Jasper Fisher, which introduces the Trojan descent motif. Caesar says that he
grieves to draw his sword against the stock of thrice
renowned Troy. The British leader, in his statement of
his claims, tells the Roman that Britons and Romans are
branches of the same Trojan root. Each act closes with
songs by the Druids that do not, however, show any very
exact knowledge of ancient British institutions, even
when judged by the standards of that time. But the
drama expresses the same national spirit as we find in
Shakespeare's historical plays:

What though the Roman, arm'd with foreign spoil,
Behind him lead the conquer'd world, and hope,

To sink our island with his army's weight. . . . .
                all our people edg'd
With Dardan spirit and the powerful name
Of country, bid us hope for victory.
We have a world within ourselves, whose breast
No foreigner hath unrevenged press'd
These thousand years. Though Rhine and Rhone can serve,
And envy Thames his never captive stream,
Yet maugre all, if we ourselves are true
We may despise what all the earth can do.

Thomas Hughes's drama, *The Misfortunes of Arthur*, presents some matters of greater interest. Its theme is similar to the tragedies of the *Mirrour*, treated in Senecan fashion. The ghost of Gorlois seeks revenge for the loss of his wife to Uther and for his death. Arthur is to lose Guinevere through the same sin of lust, and evils that grow out of the tragedy will destroy Britain. With all this we have nothing to do, but we note the familiar theme of the equality of the Britons with their Trojan ancestors:

       Lo here at length the stately type of Troy,
       And Brytain land the promist seate of Brute,
       Deckt with so many spoiles of conquered Kings, etc.

More significant is the recurrence of the prophecy. After the destruction of Arthur's kingdom and the passing of the power to the hated Saxons there shall follow a thousand years of oblivion. So, says the Ghost of Gorlois:

       Prevent not this my wreake. For you there rests
       A happier age a thousand yeares to come:

An age for peace, religion, wealth, and ease,
When all the world shall wonder at your blisse:
That, that is yours. Leave this to Gorlois ghoast.

Since Geoffrey dates Arthur's death 542, this political prophecy brings us practically to the accession of Elizabeth. The theme is elaborated in the final speech of the ghost. Now that adultery and treason are avenged, future ages are to be free, and the Britons will return under Elizabeth:

Let Virgo come from Heaven, the glorious Starre:
The Zodiac's ioy: the Planets chiefe delight:
The hope of all the yeare: the ease of Skies:
The Aires reliefe, the comfort of the Earth.
That vertuous Virgo borne for Brytaines blisse:
That piereless braunch of Brute: that sweet remaine
Of Priams state: that hope of springing Troy:
Which time to come, and many ages hence
Shall of all warres compound eternall peace.
Let her reduce the golden age againe,
Religion, ease, and wealth of former world.
Yea, let that Virgo come and Saturnes raigne,
And yeares oft ten times tolde expirde in peace.
A Rule, that eke no Realme shall euer finde,
A Rule most rare, unheard, unseene, unread,
The sole example that the world affordes,
That (Brytaine) that Renowme, yea that is thine.

This passage is in the manner of the prophecies of Merlin; it introduces, like some of those prophecies, references to the constellations; it merely states what we have met elsewhere and is one of many similar eulogies of the Queen. But some objection must have been raised to it, for we find an alternative final speech, written by William Fulbecke, which omits all references to Virgo, omits the Arthurian references, and promises an age of prosperity when Britain shall become "an Angels land." The reference is to Pope Gregory's "Angli, quasi angeli," which is Saxon, not Briton. Fulbecke's reference is to the expulsion of devils and sprites that might be called British:

> For Brytaine then becomes an Angels land,
> Both Diuels and sprites must yeelde to Angels power,
> Unto the goddesse of the Angels land.

It should be noted, also, that Fulbecke wrote an alternative speech for the introductory address of the ghost which does not contain the reference to the return of the Britons after a thousand years. We find, then, this interesting situation, that the prophecy in the first speech is omitted, and that in the final prophecy all Trojan and British references are displaced, in order to substitute a passage which is certainly not of British provenience and suggests Saxon bias. In both cases, we are told, we have "A speach penned by William Fulbecke gentleman, one of the societie of Grayes-Inne, and pronounced in stead of Gorlois his speeche penned by Thomas Hughes."

With this faint survival of the mighty battle I close this chapter. In the light of the story, it seems to me that certain modifications of current theory concerning the provenience of the Matter of Britain in the sixteenth century must be made. It is true that there was slight interest in the romantic elements in the story. Malory was read, but except for a few insignificant romances was not imitated. *Chinon of England*, the various versions of the *Amadis*, such stories as these contain some Arthurian motifs but they are not imitations or continuations of Malory. Even Spenser avoids the great knights, the great scenes and motifs of Arthurian romance according to Chretien and Malory. Sidney and his followers in the writing of the new prose fiction used a different setting, characterization, and source material.

Elizabeth's mariners sailed the seven seas, bringing back strange tales that traversed London's crooked streets. Her antiquaries searched old records, visited ruined castles and abbeys and battlefields, gathered traditions from peasant and priest, clubbed authorities, brought back to the light of day many a long-forgotten ghost. To her scholars classical antiquity was no musty record of a dead past but a revelation of surpassing interest about men almost contemporary. And her poets and dramatists drew upon all this material, and much more, for their plots. Faustus the German magician, Tamburlaine the Scythian scourge of God, Roger Bacon suspected of knowing that which it is not lawful that man should know; the strange galaxy whose deeds were recorded in the *Gesta Romanorum*, and the stranger life revealed by the Italian Doni who translated tales of the mysterious East to be Englished by Sir Thomas

North; the lives of the illustrious Greeks and Romans and the pastoral life of the Greek romances; the journalist tales of intrigue in contemporary Italy, of Catherine de Medici's traffic with the occult, and the hangman's tales of plague ridden England found in the pages of Dekker—there was never a people so eager for story, so extra-national in the curiosity to know whatever could be found out about human adventures real or imaginary, of today or of the past. Is it not amazing, then, that almost alone of the great repositories of story thus available, so little use was made of what we usually think of as the Arthurian legend? It is not that these stories were not available, for Caxton had supplied them. It is not, as has been suggested many times, and by Professor Mead only the other day, that the Puritan prejudice voiced by Ascham had weight, for Malory was read, and *Huon*, and *Amadis*, and the Greek prose tales, and Painter's *Palice*. Nor was it that Malory smacked of Popery, for Elizabethans knew how to tell old tales in terms conforming to their own tastes, and Spenser's devotion was to Holy Church, not to the Anabaptist meeting house. It is not that chivalry was dead, for throughout the Tudor period there were jousts and disguisings, and the rules of knighthood became the social standards of courtiership. Yet there is no Grail, no dramatizing or modernizing of Lancelot or Guinevere or Gawain; the Round Table stirred a bit of antiquarian interest and the Society of Archers gave its members the names of Arthur's knights, but the great themes of the cycles of romance remained untouched until a later period of Romanticism revived them, in Tennyson and his fellows.

These facts, set over against the evidence I have brought together in this chapter, enable us to draw certain rather definite conclusions.

For one thing, the Elizabethans were not interested in the Arthurian romances, that is, in the development of the legend by Chretien and his followers and redacted in part by Sir Thomas Malory. Since they drew eagerly, as I have said, upon almost every conceivable source of story, the explanation must be, in part at least, that they did not look upon the story of Arthur as we have been taught by Tennyson to look upon it, and it was this different viewpoint that gives the peculiar stamp which the Elizabethan version possesses. A very simple illustration of this is to be found, I think, in the fact that most commentators upon Spenser's Prince Arthur who have written since Tennyson's *Idylls* have been unconsciously but indubitably influenced by the conception of Arthur set forth in that work, in spite of the fact that Tennyson's Arthur differs in almost every essential respect from Spenser's. The peculiar Elizabethan stamp is, of course, characteristic of all the literature of that time; it is to be seen, for example, in North's Plutarch and in Shakespeare's use of that treasure house, to be seen also in Chapman's Homer as contrasted with Pope's or with Arnold's. But to the matter of Britain something happened that differs from the customary Elizabethan technique of translation. Chapman could have read Lancelot and Gawain as he read Homer's stories. The point is that he did not, nor did Spenser, nor Shakespeare, nor the minor writers.

To show this matter fully is a complex task, for it involves a re-examination of the *Faerie Queene* in the light of the results of the present investigation. But the clue is to be found, I think, in the peculiarly national bias that the story took with the accession of the Tudors. The Battle of the Books is one aspect of this emphasis. The antiquarians were one with Polydore in rejecting the legendary tales of Chretien and Malory, but they insisted on the historicity of Arthur and the truth of the descent from Troy. Politically, the same position was taken. Henry VII used it in support of his claims to the throne. By Henry VIII the interest was capitalized in his evident desire to be regarded as Arthur's successor, with claims that might be extended to continental Europe. For Elizabeth Tudor, there were the important matters of her right to her throne, of the ending not merely of the internecine strife of the Roses but of the chaos that followed Henry's death, and of the consequent return of the Golden Age of Arthur's reign. The question turned, therefore, upon the historicity of Arthur, not upon the quests of his knights or the endless romances that gathered about them to the virtual exclusion of the king. The Elizabethans fixed their eyes upon Arthurus Rex.

Let me try to accentuate this Tudor idea by a simple

illustration. When Geoffrey's book first appeared, Henry of Huntingdon was amazed by it, a sober and seemingly learned history containing the most astounding things, but he accepted it. At the very end of the century William of Newburgh attacked it in words some of which Polydore afterwards incorporated into his own account. At the same time Giraldus Cambrensis defended it, wrote of Glastonbury, was satisfied that Arthur was safely buried and would not return. And then for nearly three centuries little interest is apparent in the problem of historical truth, save that Higden in Chaucer's boyhood repeated William's scepticism and was printed by Caxton. Sir Edmund K. Chambers makes much of what he calls the Anglicizing of Arthur during this period. Some Arthurian elements, he observes, appear in the *ludi* of the court. Edward III made a solemn vow to re-establish the Round Table as Arthur had left it. But he was interrupted, and when the order was founded it was the Garter and not the Round Table. Again, Chambers cites Edward I as an example of this Anglicizing, for in 1301 he sought to establish his claim to Scotland by the use of evidence drawn from Geoffrey. And in Caxton's acceptance of Arthur as head of the Nine Worthies and the fact that except for Higden's no voice was raised against the king until Polydore's, he finds added proof. To me it seems, on the contrary, only proof that the dynamite concealed in Geoffrey was not yet set off. Chambers himself acknowledges that the Round Table matter was at least as apparent on the continent as in England; he does not observe the fact that by Henry VIII's time at least the Garter was regarded as an Arthurian order; his citation of the Scottish interest in the legend, in the early sixteenth century, took the form of rejecting Arthur on purely nationalistic grounds. Hector Boece is as bitter against Arthur, as I have already shown, as Polydore, but for quite different reasons. It is Scottish historical primitivism set against Tudor prejudices. Mordred was the rightful heir; Arthur was overthrown justly. And finally, Sir Edmund does not take into account what followed Polydore's attack, or distinguish between it and the scepticism of William of Newburgh or of Higden.

Against the comparative obscurity of this matter in the centuries from Geoffrey to Polydore, let us set the extraordinary energy which the legend took on with the accession of the Tudors. Is not the true explanation to be found, not in a gradual Anglicizing, but in political and historical conditions? For example, the prophecies of the return, either by the literal resurrection of Arthur or by restoration of his line, were unused from the twelfth to the sixteenth centuries, except in the numberless rebellions in Wales and elsewhere as a basis for the preposterous claims of Welsh chieftains. It is this which Shakespeare refers to in his Fluellen. It is linked with the wide-spread superstition which Sir Edmund so interestingly sets forth in his closing pages, to the effect that

Arthur, Charlemagne, Lord Kitchener, are not dead but will return.

But we have to distinguish sharply, it seems to me, between this superstition that Arthur was only sleeping, with his warriors, in this place or that in Wales, or in the North of England, or in Somerset, or Scotland, or even far-off Sicily, and the Elizabethan idea. That idea was first suggested, I believe, when Henry Tudor landed at Milford and marched under the red dragon of Cadwallader to claim Arthur's seat. Henry was not Arthur, nor was his son, nor was Elizabeth; the prophecy was interpreted mystically; in the Tudors, Arthur reigned again. So viewed, the whole process becomes clear, and may be set down in very brief space.

Let us try, then, to interpret all this story as I believe it must have appeared to a witness of Elizabeth's triumphant progress up to, say, the year of the Armada. To such an observer, it would seem that England's prosperity was due to the great gifts of the Queen for peace in religion and in international relations, and the consequent return of the Golden Age. Stirred by the mighty sequence of events, those to whom the tradition of the Roses had come down, or the Marian terror, must have felt that they had witnessed the birth of a new nation. Yet not all new, surely, but a recreation. For now the ancient Britons, descended from mighty Troy, had returned to their own. Rome was once more conquered, by a new Arthur, whose return was to be mystically expressed, a continued allegory or dark conceit.

Thus seen, the Battle of the Books is no academic ceremony but a chapter in the history of ideas. Polydore was an Italian traitor, faithful to Rome, the ancient enemy of Britain. The antiquaries who sought by their researches to overthrow him were then, if ever, in close touch with the life and thinking of the time. Their material passed instantly from the scholar's study to the court and to the people; it was seized upon by poets, by makers of masque and drama, by all patriots, and by him who was to write the epic of New Troy. Whatever may be the truth about Geoffrey's political intention when that " learned and unscrupulous old canon of St. Georges's in Oxford," to use Chambers's felicitous characterization of him, wrote his Latin history, there can be no doubt about the Tudor interpretation. How the old story thus proved, once more, its amazing generative power, has been the subject of this chapter. But we have been concerned, thus far, chiefly with tracing its power to insinuate itself in a thousand forms into the thought and emotion of the Tudor age. We are to find the place of Arthurian story in Elizabethan literature not in reprints of Malory, not in conjectures as to the damning power of Puritan malcontents, but in recognizing that here as elsewhere the Elizabethans appropriated, translated, and made their own whatever they touched. With this in mind, we may turn to a work at least co-equal in importance with that of Chretien, though on widely different lines, the *Faerie Queene.*

CHAPTER TWO

Elizabethan Fact and Modern Fancy

The conception of the *Faerie Queene* as a sustained or allegorical transcript of Tudor history into the form of romantic epic has grown with amazing rapidity in recent years, and while such interpretations are confined, for the most part, to commentary on the first and fifth books, it may be assumed that similar analysis of the remaining books is inevitable. Not only the *Faerie Queene*, which is fair game, being purely allegorical, but every work, major and minor, of the Elizabethan period is passing through the same transformation. Even Shakespeare is now held by a constantly increasing group of interpreters to have been no mere playwright but a propagandist more cunning than any recently employed by builders of battleships and more subtle than Machiavelli. Literature, in brief, is in a fair way of becoming, not matter for linguistic analysis, as opponents of the so-called Ph. D. trust have long maintained, or even documentary stuff for literary historians, but a crossword puzzle. In such a juncture, we may well recall the weighty utterance of Lord Bacon, to the effect that it is the part of wisdom ofttimes to consider the first institution of things in order to determine how far, and how wisely, modern practice has departed from ancient significance. What did the Elizabethans understand by historical allegory? What was the practice of Spenser himself? Were Spenser and Shakespeare really not poets so much as exponents of a cipher system? These questions have a far-reaching significance, transcending the mere inquiry into the interpretation of a single Elizabethan work. There is no problem of comparable importance in the entire field of Renaissance studies of the present time. In books, in scores of articles, in inquiries affecting every phase of Elizabethan literature, the trend of criticism has gone so far as to justify and require survey in order to determine, if possible, what of good and evil such investigation involves and, perhaps, to determine some canons by which the constantly increasing mass of material may be judged.

I

Let us begin such an inquiry with Spenser, first because his poetry is professedly allegorical, second because it is from the method of tracing historical allegory in the *Faerie Queene* that the application of similar methods has recently been marked in Shakespeare studies, and third because in the case of Spenser we may trace, with some precision, the current elaborate explanations of his continued or sustained allegory back to their beginnings. The most detailed exegesis of the book of Redcross is that given by Miss Lilian Winstanley (1915), who regards the story as a transcript of English history of the time of Henry VIII and Mary Tudor. Miss Winstanley, however, merely adopted, and pushed to greater extremes of identification, the views of Professor Padelford (1911), who in turn had adopted, with material additions, the conception of the allegory set forth in a paper by J. Ernest Whitney in 1888. All these interpretations agree in the theory that the first book is a romanticized history of the English reformation, the only differences being in the constantly increasing application to detail, so that not merely the general drift of the allegory, but every incident, every character in the poem is referred, with the utmost precision, to incidents and characters in early Tudor times. These Spenser commentators have not yet gone to the length of imagining the poet as looking over the shoulder of Queen Elizabeth as she wrote her letters, as has been fancied concerning Shakespeare's intimacy with the great monarch, but they are on their way. And, by implication, we have only to wait a bit longer, until the secret history of England in the sixteenth century has been thoroughly mastered, before we shall have a complete solution of the puzzle of the remaining books of the poem.

Now all this vast structure has grown out of a series of remarks concerning Spenser's historical allegory which may be quite definitely traced. For example, Professor Padelford begins his discussion by quoting some remarks found in Sir Walter Scott's review of Todd's *Spenser* in 1806. Sir Walter expressed the view that the plan of the *Faerie Queene* is much more involved than appears at first sight, and held that the poem is filled with "particular and minute allusions to persons and events in the court of Queen Elizabeth as well as to points of general history." Sir Walter, it is true, confessed a belief that ingenuity could be better employed than in trying to decipher what the poet had chosen not to leave too open, which is of course a wholly indefensible view; nevertheless, he was fascinated by what he called these "secret, and, as it were, esoteric allusions of Spenser's poem."

Scott's reference to these matters was suggested by what he found in Todd (1805), who had quoted a part but by no means all the suggestions of earlier commentators. It is to Warton (1754) that we owe at least one valuable suggestion that has not yet been systematically followed up, to the effect that Spenser's manner of allegorizing seems to have resulted rather from the influence upon him of contemporary masques than from anything he had found in Ariosto. And Warton continued with the remark that the *Faerie Queene* is " equally an historical or political poem," that, in fact, "that which is couched under this (moral) allegory is the history and intrigues of Queen Elizabeth's courtiers, who however are introduced with a moral design." It will be observed that Warton held the political and historical allegory to be of equal importance with the moral, that he regarded the chief source of this aspect of the poem to be the masques and entertainments at court; and that he regarded the history and intrigues of Elizabethan courtiers as material upon which Spenser drew. But he did not follow out his own suggestion, or attempt identifications.

This was not the case with John Upton (1758), whose rather numerous notes on the subject Todd, in his variorum of 1805, practically ignored. For example, Upton not only identified Guyon with Essex but gave, in some detail, his reasons. Spenser, says Upton, definitely states that Essex appears in the poem, and that Guyon fulfils this condition is indicated, he holds by Wotton's description of Essex as "demure and temperate." Moreover, he was raised among Puritans and was himself a Puritan; he was a member of the Order of the Garter; he was Master of the Horse to Elizabeth and Spenser stresses Guyon's horse. There is no attempt to identify the story of Guyon with events in Essex' life; Upton contents himself with quite general matters; but he holds that Whitgift, the tutor of Essex, is Spenser's Palmer. The whole theory falls to the ground, however, when we recall that Essex was a mere boy when Spenser wrote second *Faerie Queene,* and could not, by any possibility, have represented Guyon.

We find in Upton a few other similar conjectures, the most notable being his identification of Henry VIII with Redcross, in which he has been followed by later commentators. Upton's general position on the subject is found in his summary of the first book: "Where therefore the moral allusion cannot be made apparent, we must seek (as I imagine) for an historical allusion; always we must look for more than meets the eye or ear"; a remark which at once suggests its possible source in Milton.

All these theories of historical significance in the *Faerie Queene* may be traced back to John Dryden, who in 1693, in his *Essay on Satire,* stated that " the original of every knight was then living in the court of Queen Elizabeth; and he attributed to each of them that virtue which he thought most conspicuous in them; an ingenious piece of flattery, though it turned not much to his account." It is easy to see whence Dryden derived this idea, for it comes from his interpretation of Spenser's dedicatory sonnets, in which several of the distinguished men who are addressed by the poet are assured that their virtues are immortalized in the poem. Whether such a construction is justifiable, we shall see later. Here it is sufficient to point out that Dryden's casual though very positive remark, repeated with increased emphasis by a series of commentators, has led to the elaborate and detailed exegesis with which we are now so familiar. This, of course, is no new phenomenon in literary history. What was originally mere conjecture is repeated by successive historians and critics until it is received without question as fact. In the present case, the earlier identifications or supposed identifications have given way to a complex theory of historical allegory by which Spenser, having made a list of Tudor events and personages, cast them in the form of literary crossword puzzles to be unravelled by the ingenuity of later commentators.

It is necessary, then, to keep firmly in mind the fact that the whole elaborate structure of identification of character and incident in the *Faerie Queene* is wholly modern and comparatively recent, and that it is based on conjectures going no further back than Dryden. It is true that Duessa was identified, in Spenser's time, with Mary Queen of Scots. The real or pretended anger of James is a matter of record, and Jonson accepts the identification in his *Conversations with Drummond*. But we have no record of other identifications, still less of evidence that the first readers of the poem saw in it a continued allegory of Tudor history, and while the absence of such evidence is of course not conclusive, it must be taken into account.

There is no evidence, for example, of contemporary recognition of Leicester as Prince Arthur, a commonplace of modern criticism. An extreme example of the devastating influence of early conjecture is found in Cory's thesis, developed at great length in his book, *Edmund Spenser* (1917), to the effect that the later books of the *Faerie Queene* show failure of poetic power, due to the poet's disillusion when, through Elizabeth's obstinacy and, later, Leicester's death, Spenser's grandiose scheme for bringing about a marriage between the Queen and the great Earl had to be abandoned. This thesis is directly traceable to Dryden's fantastic suggestion that " Prince Arthur, or his chief patron Sir Philip Sidney, whom he intended to make happy by the marriage of his Gloriana, dying before him, deprived the poet of means and spirit to accomplish his design." Dryden's preposterous but oracular utterance, for which not a shadow of proof exists, is elevated by Dr. Cory and others, with the single substitution of Leicester for Sidney, into a key to a profoundly mistaken view of the last three books of the *Faerie Queene*. And most " literary " biographies of Spenser, such as Courthope's for example, or that by Dean Church, are built up on similar baseless conjectures transformed, by authority that rests only on constant repetition, into what purports to be fact.

II

The problem of interpretation turns upon the meaning of the word " continued " in Spenser's letter to Raleigh. That contemporary allusion has a large place in the *Faerie Queene* there can be no doubt. Moreover, there is equally no doubt of the fondness of the Elizabethans for the dark conceits, the hidden wisdom, the allegorical interpretation of poetry. Nashe conceives of all poetry as a more hidden and divine kind of philosophy. Harington reflects current views of the philosophical substratum beneath the story or history. Chapman goes even farther in his asseveration of the occult meanings, the depth of mystery in poetry, which hides, like a king his treasure and his counsels, its meaning from the vulgar. Milton praises the *Faerie Queene* because in it more is meant than meets the ear. All this, and more that might be cited, conforms to Sidney's ideas of poetry as perhaps the greatest of the learnings, a view closely analogous to that expressed in Spenser's letter.

But these hidden truths are philosophical, not of the

nature of historical paraphrase, and the historical allusions do not constitute the "continued allegory." Political doctrine as well as philosophical and moral allegory
had been found in Vergil's *Aeneid* since the Florentine
Academy, but not a transcript, into contemporary events
and personalities, of ancient story. The great debate
between the partisans of Ariosto and of Tasso turned to
a large extent upon the philosophical and moral allegory
supposed to be imbedded in the poems; Tasso, indeed,
wrote an allegorical explanation of his Godfrey, *ex post
facto*. But here, again, we find no such understanding of
historical allegory as our commentators fasten upon
Spenser's poem. Spenser belonged to the tradition of
Renaissance epic. He wrote on national origins, conforming to the advice of the Pleiade poets concerning
epic poetry; he used old words of Arthur, following the
same injunction; he discoursed of the moral virtues, of
the forming of a man in all virtuous and gentle discipline,
of the distinction between the private man and the governor, according to the interpretations of Homer, Vergil,
the Italian epics of his time. But neither in what he said
in his letter, or in the dedicatory sonnets, or in the comments on his poem that have come down from his own
time, is there any indication that he made a list of the
events of Tudor history and deliberately fitted these
events into an Arthurian romance. Such transcript of
contemporary history into the form of old legend was
made, a century later, by Sir Richard Blackmore, who
wrote epics on Arthur as Prince and as King; but Black-

more took the body of his story from Geoffrey and arranged it in such a way, and with such clear indications of his purpose, as to make clear that every person, every incident, shadowed forth persons and events in the time of William. Spenser, apparently, did nothing of the kind.

There are, of course, indications of " second intention " in many Elizabethan poems, usually poems of inferior poetic and imaginative power, and I am perfectly well aware that in such a case, for example, as Hadrian Dorrell's explanation in 1596 of the allegory of *Willobie His Avisa,* an explanation indicating only the usual Platonizing with which we are familiar, may have been deliberately planned to throw readers off the scent, and that G. B. Harrison may be right in his conjecture that the poem was a document in the Raleigh controversy of 1592-94. And I am not prepared to deny that Chapman's mystical conception of poetry as a hidden thing may have led him to such allegorizing of contemporary history as a recent Michigan dissertation presents. But in the case of Spenser we are dealing with a theory at once more naïve and more imaginative, with a structure too vast, too assimilative of a thousand sources, too patently an imitation according to Renaissance standards of the sustained epics of his own and earlier times, to credit easily the contention that the poem is a secret chronicle of Tudor history, or even more, in Miss Winstanley's theory, that it is an epic of the wars of Europe. In any case, is it not best to lay our foundation for interpretation on the facts that can be gleaned from a study of Elizabethan understanding of this form of allegory, and upon the facts, easy enough to gather, that Spenser himself supplies to us?

III

What then was the theory and practice of historical allegory in England when Spenser planned and began to write his poem?

In the first place, we may observe the origin in the masque or entertainment at court, not in Renaissance epic theory. This form of entertainment reached its zenith in the early seventeenth century; even the grave Bacon, who despised such "toys," was impelled to write an essay on masque technique. Now political allegory was a part of this technique from the beginning. Bacon himself, in his *History of Henry the Seventh*, refers to the entertainments at the marriage of Prince Arthur as being filled with astronomy, and also as being not altogether pedantical. He gave no account of them, but as we have seen the purpose of the very elaborate series of entertainments was to hail the restoration of Arthur's line in the Tudor dynasty, and to compliment the young prince, named, for political and dynastic reasons, for the great king.

Even clearer and more to our purpose is Skelton's *Magnyfycence*. This play interests us because in title and in some of its details it may have influenced Spenser, whose Arthur personifies magnificence, an epithet frequently bestowed by the chroniclers on the ancient British king, and because Henry VIII, who is the Prince in the play, was often compared with Arthur. The story is very slight, the personages are merely abstractions, tending to become types. The moral allegory is well marked, the theme being the conflict between measure or temperance and folly, and teaching that the proper management of wealth is the test of wisdom. But as Ramsay has shown there is a well-defined set of references to events in the period *ca.* 1516, the rise of Wolsey and the eclipse of Norfolk. With Wolsey, lavish in dispense, the young favorites came into power, displacing the old and wise nobility. Thus the story and the moral allegory are subsidiary to a well-marked and easily traced political purpose. If, in place of the vague abstractions of the main story, Skelton had used some episodes in ancient British history, we should have had a perfect example of story plus moral plus contemporary allegory.

A better example is found in *Gorboduc*, acted before Queen Elizabeth in 1562. Here each act is preceded by a dumbshow or pageant, which presents in symbolical form the meaning of the action; next, we have the text, and finally, the chorus which explains and enforces the meaning. The story, or plot, is taken from ancient chronicle, but is reduced to the lowest terms and is carefully explained in the general argument that precedes the whole play. The length of the acts, therefore, is due not to the amount of story but to the disquisitions of the counselors, matter excessively dull to us but of great interest to the courtiers who witnessed this dramatization of the dangers confronting a realm if careful provision for the succession should be neglected. There was no escaping the intention. Elizabeth and her ministers were given a solemn warning, through the old story, of their duty.

Here then is a clear case of ancient chronicle applied to contemporary conditions, the sort of thing that commentators hold that Spenser did in the *Faerie Queene*, and that Miss Winstanley holds was the purpose of Shakespeare in his tragedies. We may add another observation. Three courses are pointed out to the monarch: he may divide the realm between his two sons now, or he may provide for such a division at his death, or he may leave the kingdom to his oldest son upon his death, since all division is dangerous. The king chooses the first course, with resulting disaster. It is obvious that this situation is very similar to that in the story of Lear. Now suppose that Shakespeare's *Lear,* not *Gorboduc,* had been presented in 1562, or, better, suppose the play belonged to a period when the question of succession again became paramount. Using the method adopted by Miss Winstanley in her interpretation of *Othello* and *Macbeth,* we might come to the conclusion that Shakespeare wrote the play with propagandist intent. The next step would be to proceed to fit all the incidents and characters to events of the year of production. If we did not know this, it is obvious that there would be difficulty, so far as this method of interpretation is concerned, in determining whether the play belonged to the period of 1562 or to, say, 1601. That is, the fundamental question of the succession, and the characters and incidents, could be made to fit either time. Thus, by such an interpretation, we should be asked to see in *Lear* an allegorical presentation of ancient legend applied to situations supposed to be well known to the audience and a problem uppermost in men's thoughts. This is precisely what Miss Winstanley does in her analysis of *Macbeth* as propagandist material on the Scottish succession and *Othello* as what she calls the tragedy of Italy.

But there is one difficulty, and that a great one indeed. In *Gorboduc,* as we have seen, the story is subordinated to the intent, is stripped to the barest essentials, the characters are merely types, and through the dumbshow and the chorus there is no danger of failure to grasp the intention of the writers. But in *Othello, Macbeth, Hamlet, Lear,* on the other hand, we have complicated plot, complex personalities, stories utterly transcending in intensity any possible propagandist or allegorical intention. And we should not forget, moreover, that *Gorboduc* was designed for a professional audience, *Lear* for a popular audience. Even so late as 1603, Dekker supplied for his *Whore of Babylon* a dumb show to make clear the meaning of the plot.

In order to see clearly the points at issue, let us contrast the clearness and comparative simplicity of *Magnyfycence* and *Gorboduc,* or any other of a score of similar masques and dramas having allegorical or propagandist intent with Miss Winstanley's interpretation of *Lear* and *Othello.* In her *Othello as the Tragedy of Italy* (1924) she begins with the statement, undoubtedly correct, that in Shakespeare's time men habitually thought and wrote in symbols, and proceeds to develop here, as in other places, a theory of what she calls a vast contemporary mythology. Her evidence, at this point, is Pierre Mathieu's *Glorious Life and Deplorable Death of Henry IV*, 1610, in which the Gloucester plot of *Lear* is adapted to contemporary French history. The fallacy, of course, is in thinking that the fact that Shakespeare's story, in 1610, was readapted for use as an allegory of French history proves that Shakespeare intended a similar meaning. Of course it proves nothing of the kind. Even if we grant the correctness of her interpretation of Mathieu's work we should have no right to apply a similar interpretation to Shakespeare. Nor does Miss Winstanley's repeated assertion of " a vast contemporary mythology " in which France figures as an old man wandering naked in a tempest, prove that Shakespeare used any such " mythology," even if it existed, as the basis of his play. Lyly used " mythology " in his Endimion; was his " mythology " the same in meaning as that in the classical story?

In further development of her conception of " myth," Miss Winstanley cites various foreign works in which Italy is pictured as the tragic victim of the Moors, as in the *Philippics* of Tassoni in 1615. Here, although there is no story, Tassoni personifies both Venice and the Moors of Spain, and there are details that suggest his acquaintance with Cinthio, possibly with Shakespeare's play. Her list of parallels between contemporary Italian history and the incidents of *Othello* is undoubtedly impressive, and Tassoni may have seen the aptness of the story for his purpose. But it by no means follows that Shakespeare intended such an allegory. Tassoni's use of Shakespeare, granting Miss Winstanley's contention, is precisely like the use of the old chronicle in *Gorboduc,* an old story applied to contemporary conditions not within the view of the man who first wrote down the story. Any story may be so used. President Wilson, during the troubled relations between the United States and Mexico and the period preluding our entrance into the world war, was more than once compared with Hamlet: his so-called academic mind, his indecision; there were cartoons representing him as Hamlet, with the legend citing the famous lines about a time out of joint. Was Shakespeare's *Hamlet,* therefore, an allegorical prophecy of American conditions in 1916? Moreover, Miss Winstanley leans heavily upon assumptions treated as facts. There was enormous use of allegory, therefore Shakespeare must have used allegory. " Spenser," she says, " treated the epic of Europe in his *Faerie Queene;* was Shakespeare's mind less noble, or less inclusive, or less great? " To which we can only reply that no proof whatever has been given that the *Faerie Queene* is " the epic of Europe," and that even so, we need not expect Shakespeare's mind to work in precisely the same way under penalty of being considered less noble or inclusive or great.

On the other hand, Miss Winstanley is right in insist-

ing on the difference between Elizabethan psychology
and our own psychology, and in her contention that we
must endeavor to get the same angle of vision as that
from which an Elizabethan audience looked upon these
dramas. She is right, also, in emphasizing the extraordinary vogue of symbol and personification in that
period, in all the countries of Europe. To John Knox,
Mary of Scotland was a demon, an enchantress, an Acra-
sia-like incarnation of evil. Not only Elizabeth but the
courtiers were personified as deities, as knights of chivalry, as incarnation of the elements of the alchemist
philosophy. Miss Winstanley does not cite the Queen's
pet term for Burghley, " Sir Spirit," nor Petrarch's comparison of Rome to a stately woman, of venerable aspect,
but clad in mean and tattered garments, nor Poggio's
reference to her as a queen in slavery, or Raphael's letter
to Leo in 1518, in which he speaks of " the mangled
corpse of the noble matron, once the queen of the
world." It is true that such comparisons are of the stuff
of poetry in all ages: Longfellow's ship of state, Lowell's personification of the nation in his " Commemora-
tion Ode "; but there are peculiar and unique uses of
the device in Renaissance allegory, masque, drama, and
even in ordinary correspondence. This Miss Winstanley
does well to point out. But she does not take into
account the fact that even if we had a drama with such
a beautiful and stately heroine as Petrarch describes,
and even if, in such a drama, this heroine was foully
dealt with by a foreign lover, it would by no means

necessarily follow that the story should be regarded as an allegory of Rome or Venice.

Moreover, Miss Winstanley disregards, in all her work on Shakespearean tragedy, the intensity of human interest that would inevitably destroy all sense of allegory, even if such had been intended, thus defeating its own end. Her reasoning here is most peculiar. It consists in the argument that since Jonson used stock types, and Spenser used personifications, and since the masques were allegorical treatment of myth, therefore Shakespeare must have done the same thing. The fallacy is apparent in the mere statement. Spenser's Guyon, like Lyly's Endimion, is, for all the art of the poet, a type, a personification, not a person. But Hamlet is a person, and Lear, and Macbeth, and Othello. Shakespeare's method is wholly different from Spenser's. Miss Winstanley holds that Lear and Macbeth are like the old Greek tragic characters, that they are superhuman, like Dante. Quite so. And is Hamlet then James VI of Scotland because he was pedantic, averse to action, melancholy? Miss Winstanley even identifies the religion of the Ghost as Catholic, while Hamlet is a Protestant, much as Miss Rickert holds that Bottom the Weaver is James because of Scottish preëminence in weaving and because the word "bottom" means a ball of wool. It is probably true that Shakespeare went back to the old legends of Hamlet, Lear, Macbeth in order to get a freedom of treatment he could not find in the chronicles of Richard and the Henries, but this desire for greater freedom, surely, was not due to his intention of treating contemporary events, including backstairs gossip and the contents of private letters, in a continued historical allegory.

That Shakespeare was profoundly influenced by his observation of men and events of his own times I have no doubt. The great tragedies are not merely dramatized story, given intensity transcending ordinary experience by his genius, and removed from the life of his time or of any other one period. They have sources not to be traced in books or in the mechanisms of the theatre, sources in the master's own spirit, a spirit brooding on the mysteries of life and death and set in operation, as with every great artist, by the life of his time. In his introduction to his translation of the *Troades* of Euripides, Gilbert Murray points out the analogy between the events of the play and actual conditions in Athens when Euripides was writing. The correspondences are far more striking than any that Miss Winstanley advances in her allegorical interpretation of Shakespearean tragedy. But Murray insists that we do *not* have, in *Troades*, a case of political allegory. " Far from it," he says. "Euripides does not mean Melos when he says Troy, nor mean Alcibiades' fleet when he speaks of Agamemnon's. But he writes under the influence of a year which to him, as to Thucydides, had been filled full of indignant pity and of dire forebodings." Thus Gilbert Murray, writing in 1915, also " a year filled full of indignant pity and of dire forebodings," proceeds to point out the

fitness of the ancient story for reading in the crisis of his
own time. We note, first, this ancient story of the woe
of Troy; second, the use of that story by the great dram-
atist during the crisis of Athenian history; and third, the
new poignancy, to a modern reader, of the theme when
all things were again at risk. Such meanings Shakespeare's tragedies may well have had. He too reflects the
influence of great events in his own time. But this is
very far from saying that Bottom, a ball of wool, is
James the Scotsman, or that the Ghost is a Catholic, or
that since James had Bothwell excommunicated, Shakespeare conveyed knowledge of the fact to his audience by
having Hamlet refuse to kill Claudius at his prayers.

IV

Let us return from this speculative region to our
inquiry as to Elizabethan understanding and practice.
So far we have observed, in the technique of the masque
and of the definitely allegorical drama, simplicity of
character and plot, a definite guidance to the desired
application. It is, of course, possible that Shakespeare
intended some such deep and cloudy mystery as Miss
Winstanley predicates, but all that we know of his practice and character tends definitely against such an assumption. How could an Elizabethan audience, witnessing the
tragedy of Othello and Desdemona, have applied that
story to a political situation in a remote country about
which the average Elizabethan knew less than the average American of today knows of Mussolini's Italy or of

Soviet Russia? Even the courtiers, and the Queen, inordinately fond of mystifications as we know them to have been, could not have seen such transference of values as Miss Winstanley posits as the real meaning, not of one but of all of Shakespeare's great tragedies. An important corrective of all such interpretations may be found in the frequent records of Elizabeth's naïve and child-like insistence on the explanations of matters in pageants and masques which are sufficiently simple to us. What Miss Winstanley calls Elizabethan psychology is in reality her own psychology, as subjective as Goethe's interpretation of *Hamlet*. It is a new romanticism, not historical realism, that confronts us.

If we turn, now, to historical and topical allusions in Shakespeare we are on surer ground. There can be no doubt as to the significance of Macbeth's vision in the witches' cavern, of the significance, to a generation familiar with Tudor use of Arthurian story, of the escape of Fleance, who was to marry in Wales and beget future kings of Great Britain. Nor can there be any doubt of the instant reception of the allusion to Essex in *Henry V,* or of the allegory of the gardener in *Richard II* in which the long wars of Lancaster and York found momentary reference, or of the equally clear allegory of the vestal throned in the west in *Midsummer Night's Dream,* or many other topical allusions, some of which we recognize at once today, while others, known to Elizabethan audiences, now fall on deaf ears. It is possible, of course, that the passages I have cited may be key passages, giving the clue to the whole meaning of the drama in which they occur. Miss Rickert has made out a plausible case for *Midsummer Night's Dream.* I do not share Mr. Stoll's scepticism about the possible representation of the candidacy of James under the guise of Bottom, for after all James *was* an ass. But the facts that the garden allegory in *Richard II* is carefully explained and has nothing in the least subtle about it, that the allusion to Essex in *Henry V* is clearly nothing more than a topical allusion such as we find very often in present day dramas, give us pause. Allegory, even in Shakespeare who uses it but rarely, makes its presence known. And topical allusion, whether in Shakespeare or in the *Faerie Queene,* is not continued allegory, or necessarily allegory at all.

That Shakespeare's plays, or any one of them, should be interpreted as having been written for allegorical or propagandist intent, is highly improbable. Something of a case, as I have said, seems to have been made out for *Midsummer Night's Dream,* which has long been recognized as a masque-like play possibly designed for presentation on some special occasion. *Love's Labour's Lost,* as Dover Wilson holds, may also be motivated in part by the Raleigh controversy. Both plays are alike in slightness of characterization, in masque technique, and in possessing an unusual amount of what looks like topical allusion. Miss Albright has not been so successful in her efforts to attach the historical plays to the Essex problem. Her analysis of *Richard II* is marked by misuse

of evidence, by deliberate suppression, by quite unwarranted assumption, and most of all by persistent failure
to realize the real significance of the historical plays as
a group. That Elizabeth was sensitive to certain topics
is indisputably true. But a good deal of the feeling on
the part of the authorities was similar to the sensi-
tiveness about Darwinism and Bolshevism in America
today.

Courtiers must not know too much history. Fulke Greville reports that he was discouraged from attempting
to write about Tudor history because it was a dangerous
subject, but Greville was a timid man, also a lazy man;
very likely he was really seeking an excuse for not
engaging in research. At any rate others wrote of Tudor
history without trouble; Bacon said that the chief need
of his time, so far as history was concerned, was the
writing of contemporary and recent history while the
facts were still fresh in men's minds, and he made good
in part this lack by his own history of Henry VII. As
for the famous instance of Elizabeth's threat to suppress
Holinshed on the ground that it contained matter very
fondly set forth, that is nothing more than the usual
fear of getting into the public mind something better
allowed to lie in oblivion; there is no reason to believe
that Holinshed, or one of his collaborators, was suspected of deliberately shadowing forth contemporary
politics under the guise of history.

Thus the fact that the Richard II matter was felt to
be dangerous is no proof whatever that Shakespeare

wrote his play in order to preach sedition. Miss Albright's inferences are quite unwarranted. Even more extraordinary is her analysis of Shakespeare's *Henry V*. The Essex allusion is to her not mere allusion but the climax of the play. The rebellion broached on Essex' sword is not the Irish rebellion which Essex was sent to Ireland to crush, but a new rebellion, justifiable, which he is to set in motion to overthrow the old queen. Aware of the absurdity, the criminal consequences, if such a thing had been said publicly in a theatre, Miss Albright hypothecates a secret production of the play before possible and potential conspirators, for which, so far as I can see, she has not a shred of evidence. The portrait of Henry, she holds, is really of Essex. She has no evidence of this, and she quite fails to realize that while the virtues that Shakespeare praises in his hero are unquestionably the virtues of Essex in the popular imagination, they are equally the virtues of Raleigh, of Sidney, of other knights at court. The play was written, as I have said in another connection, " under the influence of the time." Harvey lists similar characteristics, cynically, necessary if one was to get on in that age of action and boldness. But Miss Albright sees in every event, every incident, even in the punishment of the rebellious lords, Essex propaganda. Again the psychology is not Elizabethan, but the neo-romanticism of this school of critics.

What we can be certain of, then, can be summed up under two heads. First, topical allusion, to persons and events, of which Shakespeare is full, like any other author of his time or any other time. Second, general passages full of meaning to his audiences, the speeches of the Bastard or of John of Gaunt for example, or Ulysses' treatment of degree. From such passages, and from others that indubitably throw light on Shakespeare's reaction to certain Renaissance ideas, as fate for example, or the nature of tragedy, or the kingship, as well as from the many topical references, we see that Shakespeare was not aloof from his time, a mere technician and fortune hunter, the man of Stratford, but was rooted in his England. He does not allegorize in *Gorboduc* fashion. He writes under the influence of his time.

V

I shall now point out, through the citation of a single work, the clue to the interpretation both of Shakespeare's chronicle plays and of Spenser's *Faerie Queene*. This work is Hall's *Chronicle,* published in 1548, and planned, as a singular mixture of romance, epic, and history, as a warning to England and an exaltation of the Tudor house. We have already found abundant evidence of the political use, by the Tudors, of the descent from Arthur. We have traced in the controversy about the historicity of Arthur, which I have called a sixteenth century battle of the books, the combination of antiquarian interest, national pride and political intention as elements in the legend. With the Tudors the Britons returned to their ancient seat. The theme caught the popular fancy, and was celebrated, in a steadily increasing current through the reign of the greatest of the Tudors, in so many pageants and dramas, so many poems, so many chronicles, as to make inevitable the conclusions I have drawn. There emerged two themes. One, the tragic story of Lancaster and York, ending in the union of England, was the theme of Hall's chronicle and of Shakespeare's historical plays. The other, the return of the ancient Britons after so many centuries, was also suggested by Hall, appears in Leland and other chroniclers, in Churchyard, Warner, and Drayton who combined chronicle with epic, and in Spenser's *Faerie Queene*. These facts, once grasped, throw a flood of light upon the interpretation of a considerable portion of distinguished Elizabethan literature, and are accompaniments of the new national consciousness which was the greatest of Tudor achievements.

In Hall, as I have said, the two themes are blended. The book was written for the glorification of the house of Tudor: " the history of Lancaster and York and the Union of England." The titles of his chapters or books prove the dramatic character of his interpretation. The influence on Holinshed, on the *Mirror for Magistrates,* on Daniel's poetry, and on Shakespeare's historical plays is unquestionable. The plays cover almost the same period; they might have used for subtitles some of the very words chosen by Hall. Mingled with the story is the constant warning of the dangers that spring from internal dissension. United, England is invincible. With the accession of the Tudors the way was open for this impregnable union that supplies the undercurrent of passionate nationalism throughout the plays. These themes also appear in the pageantry of the period, in the pageants at Elizabeth's coronation, for example. And the other theme, the return of the Britons, is equally strong in Hall. In speaking of the accession of Henry Tudor, he says: " It was by a heavenly voice revealed to Cadwallader last Kyng of Brytons that his stocke and progeny should reigne in this land and beare domynion agayn. Whereupon most men were persuaded in their same opinion that by this heavenly voice he was provided and ordeined long before to enjoye and obteine this kyngdome." And of the young prince Arthur he says: " Shortly after that to Wynchestre, where quene Elizabeth his wyf was delivered of a fayre prynce named Arthur at his baptism. Of which name Englyshmen no more rejoysed then outwarde nacions and foreyne prynces trymbled and quaked, so much was that name to all naciouns terrible and formidable."

In saying all this I do not for a moment mean to assert that Hall was the source of Shakespeare and Spenser. Far from it. He chanced merely to express, in a single work of no great length, a work which itself stands out above the flood of chronicles for its imaginative and generative power, two themes which we meet in a thousand other places, themes which are analogous to the epic ferment about which we hear in discussions of poetic origins. Both the plays and Spenser's epic thus stand as the product of widely extended Elizabethan thought; they spring from the life of their time.

But here our concern is with Spenser's treatment of the return motif, and its relation to the understanding of his allegory.

In the first place, his poem illustrates the combination of antiquarianism, national feeling, and political intention that I have shown to be the true meaning of the controversy about Arthur and the development of the matter of Arthur in Tudor England. His antiquarianism has never been sufficiently stressed. He was acquainted with Camden, admired him, and pursued at intervals throughout his life the same subjects as those followed by that prince of antiquaries. We see the results in widely scattered works: his Irish tract, for example; or in many places in his poetry; most of all in his use of British chronicle in the second and third books of the *Faerie Queene*. His national feeling was closely connected with the idea of the return of Arthur, and this is the organizing principle of the great poem. And his political intention was not to review the events of the reformation of Henry VIII but to seize upon and interpret the return motif, to show imaginatively the qualities of the golden age of chivalry, and, most of all, to lay bare, through masque and allegory, the hidden dangers that threatened the realm and to exalt the strengths able to overcome these perils.

Even in this last matter, so closely bound up with the interpretation of the allegory, Spenser was not original. He found his virtues and vices, his allegory, his mas-

ques, equally with his return motif, in the pageants and
the literature of his time. Since his poem was to honor
Elizabeth the Queen of Faerie, it is fitting that he should
have linked it with the pageants that she loved and with
themes sung by poets not once only but on each anniversary of her accession. Dr. Heffner, in a paper read
before the English Seminary at Johns Hopkins, and
recently printed in *Studies in Philology,* subjected the
pageants presented at Elizabeth's coronation, and the
anniversary poems that followed, to a critical study.
He found in them many reasons for supposing that the
emphasis on religious reform, the theme of the first
book of the *Faerie Queene,* was not interpreted by Spenser's audience as the achievement of Henry VIII, the
usual position of interpreters of the allegory of this
book, but as the first and greatest achievement of the
Queen. Elizabeth was the true heir of Henry VIII. In
the coronation pageants satire of cardinals and bishops
aroused the ire of foreign legates. These legates understood the vices, symbolically apparelled, as referring to
Mary's reign; Spenser's Duessa is Mary Tudor, who had
led astray Red Cross and brought back, temporarily, the
terror of the dragon of Rome. In the pageants, also,
Elizabeth is identified as *Religio Pura.* Truth, clad in
white, is brought forth by Time. The masque presented
at the coronation suggests in many ways Spenser's
method: the technique of chivalry; the contest between
vices and virtues, both of these being treated not in
Aristotelian manner but in Spenser's manner; the blend-
ing of moral allegory with political intention.

In other pageants and poems we find celebrated what was described as the principal service of the Queen: " The long desired unity which (God and her Majesty be thanked) is knit betweene us and the holy gospell." And such works as Hayward's *Annals,* Niccols's *England's Eliza,* Dekker's *Whore of Babylon,* and Lever's *Queene Elizabeth's Teares* (1607) further evidence popular interest in such things as Spenser treats in his poem: Elizabeth's sufferings at the hands of Gardiner before she became queen; her first care to re-establish religion; her contest with error and with the dragon of Spain. This evidence is so considerable in amount, and recurs with such frequency in writings scattered through the years of her reign, as to give grounds for feeling that the usual reference of Spenser's first book to the period of Henry VIII is open to serious question. Stated simply, the proper interpretation of this evidence would seem to be that we are not to look for a continued historical allegory, in which each event in Spenser's story shadows some event in Henry's reign and each character stands for some one who figured in the history of that prince, but that we are to read this first book as a reflection of the popular interpretation of conditions at Elizabeth's accession, and popular recognition of her first great service in the cause of truth. It seems reasonable enough. After all, Spenser's poem is entitled the *Faerie Queene,* and, if so, why should we suppose that he began by writing an allegorical history of the reign of her father?

But the true approach to an understanding of the method and purpose of the *Faerie Queene* is to be found, I think through a study of the second book. It is one of the great books, in which all sides of Spenser's method and art are represented. It is exactly parallel, in structure, to the first book, and without question the two books were designed by the author to complement each other and to present his fundamental thought. The virtue which it represents is temperance, self control, governance through the rational faculty of the soul which is warred on by wrath and sensuality. The political intention of the book is as plain as that of the companion book.

Here again we gain some light from contemporary literature, and this should be the method of approach rather than, as heretofore, through discussion of the Aristotelian aspects of the philosophy. Out of many illustrations I shall here cite but one, of value to us because it shows once more Elizabethan understanding of political allegory and deals with matters treated by Spenser in this second book.

In 1562 a meeting between Elizabeth and Mary of Scotland was projected, in an effort to bring about an understanding. The meeting did not take place, but we have much material bearing upon the plans, including a full account, in Burghley's handwriting, of the entertainment " to be shewed before the Queenes Majestie, by waye of maskinge." The author of the masque is unknown, but its importance to Burghley's plans for the conference is indicated by the fact that he wrote out a full abstract with his own hand. A prison (Oblivion) is represented, its jailer being Argus or Circumspection; the symbol of two hands clasped, with a motto, "Faith" in gold. Then come two women, one on a gold lion with a gold diadem, representing Prudence, and the other on a red lion, also with a diadem, representing Temperance. Several ladies bring in, as prisoners, Discord and False Rumor. Pallas presides over the court, enjoining the virtues to declare to the two queens (Elizabeth and Mary) that the two virtues Prudence and Temperance had long prayed Jove to punish False Rumor and Discord for taking their place. The vices are shut up; Prudence gives the jailer wands with inscriptions indicating everlasting banishment to oblivion. There is little or no speaking, the whole being much like the dumb shows we have already noted in *Gorboduc.*

On the second night the setting is a Castle of Abundance; the virtues are Peace and Amity. Several ladies, as before, are introduced; there are explanatory verses to make the intention clear. Amitie announces to the queens that Pallas had shut up the vices, the subject of the masque of the preceding night. The gods having learned that Prudence and Temperance are to remain at the Court of Plentie have sent Peace to stay also. Ardent Desire serves Prudence; Perpetuity serves Temperance; through these eternal Peace shall reign. The entertainment is to be followed by dances in which

English men take as partners Scottish dames. On the third evening a double masque was to have been presented. Evil Thought appears on a serpent and accompanied by Disdain brings a message from Pluto resenting the punishment of False Rumor and Discord and stating that a champion has been sent to right the wrong. Discernment enters with a horse on which rides Valiant Courage, sent by Jove against the demons Disdain and Evil Thought. Victory, we are told, is not possible unless Prudence and Temperance make an alliance with Peace. This done, Discernment lays a large sword at the feet of the two queens and the demons are driven back to hell.

Here then we have an allegorical masque, of political intention, strikingly similar in setting and import to the sort of thing we find in Spenser. It is not, of course the source, but the characters are the same. Temperance and Prudence in the masque resemble Guyon and the Palmer in Spenser's treatment; Discord, False Rumor, Disdain, the emblematic animals, all correspond closely to Spenser's characters in this book and in the closely allied fourth book, dealing with Friendship or Concord. The court, the trial, the warfare on the virtues (analogous to the siege of Alma's Castle in the Legend of Temperance), the interposition of the infernal deities— all this is of the stuff found in Spenser's poem. Moreover, by observing how these elements are combined in the masque and the purpose of the writer, we can determine the bases of Spenser's method, because in the masque matters are presented in the simplest form, the bare kernel of thought and intention, which Spenser embellishes, lifts from the simple teaching of a masque to a highly decorated and complex piece of Renaissance poetry. Moreover, Temperance is presented in the masque, as in many other places which might be cited, as a political virtue.

It has seemed easy, so often has the theory been advanced, to attach specific events to the story of the first book; but students have been puzzled when they have attempted, in pursuance of the conventional theory of continued allegory, to do the same thing with the second book. The error, I am persuaded, in both cases has been due to a misapprehension of Elizabethan practice and Spenser's intention. We might, for example, apply the conventional method to the masque which so interested Burghley because of its political possibilities. We might identify Discord, False Rumor, Discernment, the embassy from Pluto, the challenge to the queens. We might see in Argus the jailer the guardianship of the great Lord Treasurer himself. But is it not perfectly clear that no such intention was in the mind of the author of the masque? A quarter of a century before the tragedy of the two queens was to end in the execution of the one by the other, the dangers to the realm were clearly grasped by Burghley and perhaps by the great actors themselves, and this attempt was made to see if accommodation could not be reached. What might have been presented as a state paper, or made the matter of negotiation, was here presented simply, objectively, through the masque. Simple and clear as the story was, one that apparently the queens themselves and the courtiers could have understood without difficulty, the author supplied careful explanations of his intention. Allegory, as I have said before, makes its presence felt, and supplies clues to its interpretation. In the light of these observations, what becomes of the elaborate crossword puzzles with which modern commentators have sought interpretation of Spenser's poem and are now seeking interpretation of Shakespeare's plays? Spenser's Temperance, like his Holiness, was a political virtue, and the main lines of his story are applicable, in a wholly simple and understandable manner, to techniques familiar to Elizabeth and her court. There is allegory, but it is not a continued and systematic transcript of history.

More detailed analysis of the historical allegory, with attention to the numerous instances of contemporary allusion, may be reserved for another place. The ethical allegory is more marked in the second book than in the first, which is doctrinal, and this allegory, as I have shown in another place, unites elements from Aristotle and Plato. It is worth noting that Aristotle gives high place to temperance as a political virtue in the seventh book of his *Politics*. But the basis of Spenser's doctrine, in its political side, is the interpretation given to the queen's course with reference to the dangerous conditions that confronted her. The nation needed concord, temperate handling of vexed questions, relief from the fanaticism of Bloody Mary. This Elizabeth gave, guided by Burghley, and that her wisdom was recognized by her subjects is proved by the frequent association of her name with these virtues of the golden mean. The book of Guyon is devoted to this theme. The enemies are discord and violence, and seductive ease. Archimago, the chief fomenter of discord, plies his trade unceasingly. Acrasia, who owes much to Tasso's enchantress, is set over against Alma and is sent as prisoner to Gloriana as Alma is defended by Arthur. Through it all is the evil of civil anarchy, and the need for national unity above every other consideration. The Anglican movement was not doctrinal but national. The praise of England, her strength to repel all foreign invasion if only internal dissension should be stamped out, the identification of the Tudor monarch with the state, Elizabeth's right through her ancestry to the throne (the chronicles), and the chief dangers which threaten her are the themes set forth in Book II.

Up to this point it seems fairly clear that Spenser had abundant precedent for his use of holiness, temperance, concord, and similar virtues as political virtues. This single observation disposes of the various attempts to shut him within a rigidly Aristotelian system, in which his first virtue, holiness, has no appreciable place. It disposes also of the vain attempts to impose upon him, as a definition of his continued allegory, the necessity of converting English chronicles beginning with the reign of

Henry VIII into a consistent and chronologically contin-
uous allegory. And, most of all, it indicates that Spenser
was lifting into the realm of literature an attitude, a
technique, a mode of thinking that is exemplified a
thousand times in the records we have of Elizabethan
practice. The *Faerie Queene* gains immeasurably, I
think, by such a conception. We have become accus-
tomed to realizing, as former generations did not, the
impossibility of understanding a poem like Dante's
Divine Comedy, for example, without intimate knowledge of such a background in Dante's world. The most
recent commentary on Dante devotes the entire first
volume exclusively to this background, a treatise based,
let it at once be said, not on the application of " taste "
or any other pseudo-humanist conceptions, but upon the
results of minute research in which many scholars have
collaborated, each one bringing his own small contribution. Milton's *Areopagitica,* less imposing than Dante's
poem or Spenser's, has recently been shown to be but
one of many similar discussions, beginning in a specific
problem of interest to the time, lifted by Milton's genius
out of the temporal into an ever-living defence of truth.
So it was with Spenser. We are not to see, in the Coronation pageants or in the projected masque of 1562,
sources, in the usual sense of that much abused term.
We see through them how the court circle looked upon
such matters. They are like editorials and critical articles written about some modern statesman or some public cause, enabling a later generation to know how men

and matters looked to contemporaries, instruments to understanding.

VI

There emerge, then, certain simple facts:

1. Allegory of the special type we are here considering is simple, makes its presence known, has a general rather than a minute application.

2. When, as momentarily in Shakespeare and far more frequently in Spenser, it refers to specific persons or events, this reference is by way of illustration or compliment or ornament, never sustained for long, never based on an intimacy of detail which the modern student may perhaps derive from his study of documents now available but in Elizabethan times secret, known to few, matters of highly confidential correspondence. History in the making, it is well to remember, is never so simple, so capable of ordered narrative and interpretation, as it appears to a later generation.

3. Keeping these two principles in mind, we recognize certain contemporary topics, interpretations, and beliefs, commonplaces of Elizabethan thought. Among these are the national feeling that the queen's first great service was the re-establishment of religion. Redcross, to speak in Elizabethan terms, has been led astray, the maiden Truth has been deserted and placed in dire peril, but through the spirit of ancient Britain and the ministrations of true religion, Duessa is put to flight and the dragon is slain. This is the substance, purely

Elizabethan, of the first book, as it is the substance of masque and drama and of poems in praise of England and her sovereign. Into the second book, in turn, is woven the popular conception of the second great trial of the queen. Restraint, temperance, reason, unity against the enemies of an ordered government supply the theme. But it is no mere abstraction, this virtue of temperance. A new element, of great importance, is added to the pale and bloodless abstractions of the masque.

Let us consider the rôle of Arthur in the two books. In the first, he rescues Redcross from the dungeon into which he has been plunged in consequence of his own folly. Now Redcross is no fairy but a changeling, in charge of fairies, not Briton but Saxon born. Arthur is Arthur of Britain. The story of Truth, brought to straits by the defection of her knight, is perhaps faintly reminiscent of the sufferings of Elizabeth the princess. Rescued by Arthur, comforted by the princess, Redcross recovers his lost sense of spiritual values and is enabled, after a period of preparation, to slay the dragon. Arthur here may symbolize, as has been often said, the truth that the single virtue is powerless in great emergency unless helped by Magnificence, sum of all the virtues. Or he may, more reasonably, represent the old device familiar in romance technique, of having the greatest knight in the world, Lancelot or another, appear in a story in which a new and untried knight is the titular hero. Spenser's art is complex, compound of many simples; both these conceptions may have been in his mind. But the great conception, the one that goes to the root of his real thought, is bound up with the widespread interest in the return motif. England is saved by the interposition of Arthur the Briton.

With this in mind we pass to the much greater rôle of Arthur in the second book. To Guyon he re-tells his vision of the Faerie Queene and the object of his quest. With Guyon he defends Alma's Castle, takes part in the events leading to the final great adventure, is co-hero in all the principal actions of the book (Cantos viii-xi). And with Guyon in the pivotal section of the entire story, the period of preparation, of withdrawal, of contemplation before the great task is finally entered upon, he secures strength and insight from the study of the records of his people.

It was long the fashion to speak contemptuously of the chronicle material thus introduced by Spenser. Running out of fresh invention, critics have said, he inserted youthful work. Or he imitated Vergil and epic convention generally, by the device of the vision of history introduced to compliment the reigning house. The interpolation, which literary critics profess themselves unable to understand or to justify, was a blemish, to be avoided by the reader in search of the beauties of Spenser, subject for pedantic research, not humanistic in its aims.

So be it. I am not careful to answer in this matter. But the fact remains, whatever critics may feel, that

Spenser put this material into a place which we know he considered pivotal, essential to the understanding of his plan. This chronicle material was subjected, some years ago, to careful study by Miss C. M. Harper. It was a typical Ph. D. subject, according to the views of our humanists: small, of no value, something that industry without intelligence might solve. But Miss Harper found out, by the only possible means by which such things are ever found out, that is by patient research and parallel studies, that Spenser's chronicle is no mere prentice work. He did not get up the subject by reading some standard work and converting it into his stanzas. He read many sources. He brought to bear what critical historical sense he possessed, in his use of his authorities. He used many sources. It was the product of long and intense study.

Based on the evidence that Miss Harper has given us, we may assert that Spenser was as close a student of the historical aspects of the story of Arthur as any of those who took part in the controversy. We have seen the special significance of the Arthurian matter in Tudor times. What we are now in a position to observe is that this chronicle of Spenser's is not only evidence of his antiquarian interest and careful study, but is itself a document in the great quarrel. It is a defense of the historicity of Arthur. It is a compliment to the Tudor house, but it is also something far more significant. Like Camden, Spenser subscribes to a belief in the value of this antiquarianism to the development of national spirit. So Arthur, confronting a crisis, derives strength and faith not from holy church, like Redcross, but from the history of his people.

In some such manner, I believe, we must approach the vexed problem of Spenser's political intention. The virtues are those that seemed, not to Spenser alone but to the English people, incarnate in their queen. That he should speak of them as Aristotelian in origin and twelve in number offers no difficulty. There was common knowledge of Aristotle, his ethics and his politics; and in the seventh book of the *Politics* Aristotle had stressed temperance as a major virtue. But in Spenser and his time it was a diffused Aristotelianism that was influential; we do not find in the *Faerie Queene* a systematic translation of the ethics any more than we find in it a systematic but concealed contemporary history. The first achievement of the queen was the restoration of religion; the next was the establishment of a settled government by routing Discord, Guile, Zeal and all fanaticisms, the lure of the irrational and intemperate. These basal idealisms, themes treated in a large body of Elizabethan writings, Spenser built into his poem, built into it, also, the great theme of the return of the house of Arthur and the restoration of ancient British glory.

What then has become of the theory of a continued historical allegory? It has disappeared, like the false Florimel. For it was based on misapprehension that has grown since the time when Dryden misread the dedicatory sonnets. There is political and contemporary

allusion aplenty, and persons and events in contemporary affairs appear often enough. For it is of the essence
of Spenser's Platonism that the perfect idea, the ·ideal
virtue, should be incarnated now in one and now in
another person belonging to that brilliant court. So
Arthur may very well be Leicester on occasion, but not
Leicester throughout the poem; Arthegal may be Lord
Grey in a part of the fifth book, but not Lord Grey
through all his story; Calidore may represent, at different times, Essex as well as Sidney. This is what Spenser
meant by saying to some of the courtiers addressed in
his dedicatory comments, that their heroic qualities are
preserved in his poem. Some of these impersonations
we recognize, not all. And some of the events, where
needed for ornament or illustration, or for high praise
or blame, also are imbedded in his narrative. But again,
not all. Else why do we not have the massacre of 1572
in France, which so highly moved Leicester and Sidney,
men whom Spenser followed? Why do we not have the
martyrdoms of the earlier period, chief influence,
according to some historians, in bringing on the Reformation? Such themes were well known and often used, by
other writers. They would not have required the subtlety of interpretation or the access to private sources
drawn upon by those moderns who are bent on con-
structing for the poem a continued historical allegory.

This over-subtlety, this conception that the entire tor-
tuous diplomacy of the government was matter of common knowledge and interpretation, is the fundamental

objection to the method of interpretation that I am here reviewing. We constantly expect too much. An old chronicler, Thomas Heywood, tells of an incident in the life of Edward VI, in 1552. On St. George's Day the young king came from church with all the nobility " in state correspondent for this day (and) said, My Lords, I pray you what Saint is S. George, that wee so honour him heere this day? The Lord Treasurer made answer, If it please your Maiesty, I did neuer in any History read of S. George, but onely in Legenda aurea, where it is thus set doune, that S. George out with his sword and ran the Dragon through with his speare." Whereupon the King, " hauing sometime vented himselfe with laughing, replyed, I pray you my Lord, and what did hee with his sword the while? That I cannot tell your Maiesty, said hee." And old Heywood, who tells us the story, sputtering, we may imagine, with indignation, prints in his margin: " He that shall but peruse the History of S. George now written by M. Heylin, may soone goe beyond the L. Treasurers answer to the King."

The incident is illuminating. We attribute too much, not merely to the varied audiences who looked upon Hamlet and Othello, but to dignitaries like lord treasurers and even monarchs. Elizabeth's own reactions to the pageants and masques presented for her entertainment were often naïve almost beyond belief. What would she have said, had she been compelled to read Miss Winstanley's exposition of the first book of the *Faerie Queene,* or her theory about Othello and Desdemona, or Miss Albright's theories about the careful marshalling of the Essex plot by William Shakespeare?

In the face of such difficulties, the only safe course to follow is to begin with assumptions which we know, with reasonable certainty, to have been truly Elizabethan. The results are tentative, not yet certain, but they are based upon a method wholly different from that which is responsible for the exaggeration of so much present day writing on the subject. The error in the conventional method becomes clear the moment we consider how it came into being. Dryden led the way by suggesting the game and its quarry. Various guesses were made in the eighteenth century; some are still repeated as fact; for others substitutions have been made. But always the method has been that of solving a puzzle. The text is read; a person is assigned; his life and deeds are applied to the text. Latterly, chronological events, major and minor persons, even bushes and trees, have been fitted into preconceived hypotheses. It is not the method of science, but of the crossword or jigsaw puzzle.

For such a method we must substitute one that starts from no preconceived notion of what Spenser might or should have done, but from certain rather simple conceptions, based on ascertained fact, and from these proceeds to inquire, so far as may be possible after so many years, concerning the historical allusions, the topical elements, which are the ornaments and graces, not the underlying structure, of the *Faerie Queene*.

CHAPTER THREE

SATIRE AND CONTEMPORARY ALLUSION

The most critical year in the life of Spenser was that extending from the summer of 1579, when he was preparing for the publication of the *Shepheards Calender,* to the summer of 1580, when he went to Ireland as the secretary of Lord Grey. The epistle to Harvey, prefixed to the *Calender,* was dated " from my lodging at London thys 10. of Aprill, 1579 "; but the book was not published until some time in the following winter. Besides this, his first ambitious work, Spenser had various other literary undertakings in hand, including a first draft of the great epic. By the tenth of April, 1580, he was anxious to have Harvey's judgment on the *Faerie Queene,* and on the twelfth of August he landed in Ireland.

The most important document bearing on this period is the letter to Harvey dated October fifth. This letter has been frequently cited for its discussion of reformed versifying; but the real significance has, I believe, been strangely overlooked. It is true that much space is given to telling about the Areopagus, and there are some specimens of Spenser's lamentable essays in the new versification; but these are merely incidental to his real purpose, which was to ask Harvey's advice on some matters on which he was in doubt. " My principal doubts are these," he says. " First, I was minded for a while to have intermitted the uttering of my writings; leaste by over-much cloying their noble eares, I should gather a contempt of myself, or else seeme rather for gaine and commoditie to doe it, for some sweetnesse that I have already tasted. Then also, me seemeth, the work too base for his excellent Lordship, being made in Honour of a private Personage unknowne, which of some ylwillers might be upbraided, not to be so worthie, as you know she is: or the matter not so weightie, that it should be offred to so weightie a Personage; or the like."

That this passage refers to the *Calender,* and that Spenser was considering a dedication to Leicester, there can be no doubt. The " private Personage unknowne," who, though " worthie," is yet celebrated in the " base " style of a pastoral, is certainly Rosalind. The facts that the prefatory letter to Harvey was dated April tenth, and that when the *Calender* appeared it was dedicated to Sidney, offer no difficulties. By October, Spenser had been received with so much favor by Leicester that he contemplated offering his poem to the powerful favorite, and sought Harvey's advice. This is the real occasion for his letter. It is also in this same letter that Spenser speaks of Gosson's impudent dedication of the *School of Abuse* to Sidney, "being for his labour scorned "; he continues, " Suche follie is it, not to regarde aforehand the inclination and qualities of him to whome wee dedicate oure Bookes. Suche mighte I

happily incurre entituling *My Slomber* and the other
Pamphlets unto his honor. I meant them rather to
Maister Dyer."

There is yet more of importance in this letter. Spenser speaks of his intimacy with Sidney, and proceeds:
"Your desire to heare of my late beeing with her
Maiestie, muste dye in itselfe. As for the twoo worthy
Gentlemen, Master Sidney and Master Dyer, they have
me, I thanke them, in some use of familiarity." And
near the end, after asking Harvey to write the news
when Spenser has gone abroad, he continues, "As gentle
M. Sidney, I thanke his good Worship, hath required of
me, and so promised to doe againe."

Thus far it is evident that Spenser was elated over his
relations with Leicester, Sidney, and Dyer; that he was
proceeding with caution, though inclined to dedicate
the *Calender* to Leicester, because fearful of presuming
as Gosson had presumed with Sidney; and that his present position was of such importance that he had been
sent to the Queen on confidential business. But the
most significant passage is that in which he shows that
even literature is of secondary importance:

"I was minded also to have sent you some English
verses: or Rymes, for a farewell: but by my Troth, I have
no spare time in the world, to thinke on such Toyes,
that you know will demaund a freer head, than mine is
presently. I beseech you by all your Curtesies and
Graces let me be answered ere I goe: which will be, (I
hope, I feare, I thinke) the nexte weeke, if I can be

dispatched of my Lorde. I goe thither, as sent by him, and maintained most what of him; and there am to employ my time, my body, my minde, to his Honours service."

The true significance of this letter consists not in its discussion of Areopagus and reformed versifying, or even in the list of poems which Spenser had ready for publication, but rather in the tone of hope, in the sense of his having established important relations with men who could advance him, in the extreme caution naturally felt by a young man who does not wish to make a nuisance of himself; in short, in the very clear impression which it gives that, for the moment at least, his head was full of more important matters than verse-making, and that his poetry was mainly valuable as a means to worldly preferment.

If we turn, now, to the third of these " Three Proper and wittie familiar letters," dated in April, 1580, the change in tone is marked. The letter is purely literary. Spenser treats of quantity and accent, giving illustrations; seeks to compare Harvey's theories with Drant's; speaks of his literary undertakings, naming several poems. Evidently Harvey's prophecy had come true: something had occurred to turn the poet back to his visions and his books. In August he was in Ireland, beginning the long period of exile, and deprived of his hopes of rising in the councils of state. I wish to stress these points, even at the expense of repetition: In October, Spenser was at Leicester House, intimate with the

powerful group of men about the great earl, confident
of preferment; by the following April, he had turned
once more to literature. In August he was in Ireland,
the dream over. I propose now to offer an explanation
of these circumstances.

I

Before I discuss the possible relations of two important poems to this passage in Spenser's life, it is necessary to treat briefly the crisis which confronted Leicester
in 1579-80. At no other time in the history of this
most powerful of Elizabeth's favorites was he engaged
in such a battle as confronted him when the queen
seemed about to marry the duc d'Alençon. Not even
the critical period 1585-86, when Leicester aroused the
fury of his mistress by assuming the lordship of the
States, can compare with this; for in 1585 he had given
up all hopes of ever becoming the king-consort. In
1579, it is very certain, such hopes still remained.

Early in 1579, the Queen's marriage with Alençon
again seemed imminent. Jehan de Simier, master of the
wardrobe for the duke, arrived early in January, and at
once became the favorite of the Queen. He is described
as " a consummate courtier, steeped in the dissolute gallantry of the French Court." His correspondence with
the Queen is of a frankness, an intimacy, which is as-
tonishing, even for the times. Elizabeth had already had
experiences of a tender nature with La Mole (1570),
an earlier ambassador, but La Mole was an amateur in
love-making in comparison with the artful Simier. He

at once became her "monkey." In February, Talbot
writes of her continued "very good usage of Monsieur
Simier and all his company," and says, "she is the best
disposed and pleasantest . . . that is possible." Castelnau writes to Catherine that not a day passes that the
Queen fails to send for him, or to visit him, at times
before he is dressed; "those who are against it are
cursing him, and declare that Simier will cheat her, and
has bewitched her." Leicester became violently jealous,
and endeavored to prevent the Queen from signing the
passports for the coming of Alençon at the end of June,
but he was defeated by Simier. In August, the prince
came, and from the first day was the Queen's "frog."
Alençon, being not less expert in love-making than La
Mole and Simier, was in the highest favor, and the
Queen seemed completely bewitched, while the Puritan
pulpits fulminated in vain against the unholy alliance,
and Elizabeth's subjects talked of love philtres and
black art as the secret of the hold the two Frenchmen
had obtained. But the crisis came in October. From the
second to the eighth of that month, the Queen's council
met daily. At length the final responsibility was left to
Elizabeth. She wept, railed at her faithful servants,
exiled some of them; even her faithful "sheep," Hatton,
was in disgrace. Stubbs's book, "The discovery of a
gaping gulph, whereunto England is like to be swallowed by another French marriage, if the Lord forbid
not the bans, by letting her Majesty see the sin and punishment thereof," discloses the temper of the people,

though the daring author was disgraced and lost his right hand. The clergy were put under restraint by a proclamation. Only Sidney dared to protest directly to her Majesty, and his frank and manly letter reflects credit on him.

It is beside our purpose to enter into a complete discussion of this complicated intrigue. Probably the real crisis in the Queen's mind was passed by the time Simier left, in November. But that she was on the very verge of marriage and that her heart was deeply affected, there can be no doubt. The next year the affair came up at intervals, reaching the second crisis in November, 1581, when the Queen publicly kissed Alençon and told her friends that he was to be her husband. Without doubt, her council believed her, excepting Burghley, who by this time saw clearly the game she was playing, and possibly Leicester. In the case of the earl, however, his own love for the Queen, not yet dead, led him to distrust her, and he showed his mad jealousy at times by secluding himself, at other times by conniving at the assassination of Simier, and at times even by plotting with the Spanish ambassador to make the match impossible.

Outwardly the relations of Burghley and Leicester were friendly. Still, we must remember that the Queen would have married Leicester long before if the great treasurer had not prevented. That the earl knew this, one feels certain. As was his custom, Burghley sought to gain his ends by keeping in the background. I find it very difficult to determine his real attitude toward the marriage. As an Englishman, with Puritan leanings, he probably detested the idea as much as any one could. But he saw more clearly than others the extreme danger of England's position. Mary of Scotland was a source of alarm; if the Catholic powers joined to put her on the throne, Elizabeth was lost. One must confess that Burghley was actuated by far-seeing motives, while Leicester was impetuous, short-sighted, selfish. One is also quite sure, on reading the reports of council meetings and studying with care those very interesting tables which Burghley was in the habit of drawing up, that to Leicester, Sidney, Hatton, Walsingham and others, Burghley seemed in favor of the marriage. His action was fox-like. Probably he hoped the game might shape itself so that the Queen might avoid the marriage; certainly he carefully avoided closing the negotiations, but rather helped the Queen to keep her suitor, and of course her followers, in perpetual hot water. One who reads these records constantly feels that Leicester was, with reason, suspicious of Burghley, while Burghley, in turn, realized that the powerful earl was a dangerous adversary.

As to Leicester himself, he blew hot and cold. At times he openly favored the negotiations. At these moments he appears to have been sure that it was all a drama, that Elizabeth would find a way out. But of his personal jealousy of Alençon and Simier, especially of the latter, there is no doubt. It was in August of 1579, after an attempt to kill Simier had failed, that Simier launched his thunderbolt by revealing Leicester's marriage. As is well known, it was always dangerous to tell the Queen of the marriage of one of her favorites. She liked to be surrounded by a circle of tame animals. Her rage knew no bounds; the earl came near losing his life, and he had no cause to love Simier.

II

We have now to consider an extraordinary characteristic of Elizabeth's relations to her followers, which will help to explain Spenser's connection with the whole intrigue. It was a whimsical custom with the Queen to give her admirers the names of animals. Thus, Simier was her " ape "; Alençon, her " frog "; Hatton, her " sheep." Leicester seems to have been known as the " lion " or the " bear "; more frequently he was her " sweet Robin." Other names were " spirit " or " leviathan," for Burghley; " dromedary," for Egerton; " boar," for Oxford; " Moor," for Walsingham. The letters of the time are filled with illustrations of these and other pet names. With his usual adaptiveness, Simier not only rejoiced in his name of " singe," but devised a code for use in his correspondence with the Queen. By this code, the king of France was known as " Jupiter " or " Mars " or " Mercure "; Elizabeth was " le soleil," " la perle," " le diaman "; the king of Spain was " la ronse " or " Vulcan "; Orange was " le guanon " or " le pigon "; Montmorency was " le faucon "; Casimer, " le corbeau " or " l'estourneau "; Bi-

ron, " le renard "; Bellegard, " le grifon "; Matignon,
" la perdris "; Anjou, " le loryer " or " l'olivier "; and
the Queen of Navarre was " la lune," " la rose," " le
rubis." One cannot be sure how widely known these
code-names were; probably Burghley and Leicester
knew them; but the point which I wish to stress is that
the custom of using animal names was highly characteristic. Even more interesting is Simier's constant use
of such phrases as " nonbre de vos bestes." Perhaps as
significant an example as any is in a letter which seems
to beg the Queen to protect him from the fury of Leicester: " Je vous requiers & vous suplye très-humble-
ment que le singe soit toujours continué au nonbre de
vos bestes, & qu'il vous playse le conserver de la pate
de l'ours." In another letter he writes, " Je ne vous dis
pas cela sans cause, vous suplyent très humblement,
Madame, me continuer de vos faveurs autant que la
moindre de vos bestes, & la plus affectionée de toutes le
peut mériter; vous assurent que je ne veus conserver
la vye de vostre singe que pour vous en fere ung sacri-
fice." A third example, from a letter of the same
period: " J'ay prins ung peu de courage, et ayent overt
vos deulx lectres qu'il vous a pleu m'escripre, je recog-
neu à mon grand regret que vostre maté avoit quelque
mescontantement de seluy qui ne veut et ne peut vivre
ung car d'eure s'il ne se voit continuer au nonbre de vos
bestes, et en la qualité de singe, puis qu'il vous a pleu
ainsi le noumer." And again: "Asures vous sur la foy
d'un singe, la plus fidelle de vos bestes, que vostre

grenoule se nourit d'espérance qu'il a que vos envoyes bien tost guérir les conmiseres, pour mestre la fin qu'il désire " etc.

Instances might be multiplied indefinitely. Catherine de Medici is called, repeatedly, " Mad. de la Serpente." Simier is constantly calling himself the Queen's " pauvre singe "; Alençon thanks her for good offices of which he hears from " nostre singe "; the ape prostrates himself before her, " car je suis vostre singe, et vous estes mon créateur, mon deffançeur, mon adjuteur, et mon sauveur," etc.; the " frog " cannot sleep for weeping and sighing, and the " monkey " takes the liberty of humbly kissing her lovely hands.

These, then, are the conditions in this strange year 1579-80. The Queen, madly infauated with her " ape " and her " frog," adepts in love-making and compliment mongering, is in danger of letting her affections run away with her judgment. Burghley is thought by court and country to favor the match, while Leicester, madly jealous, yet fearful, blows hot and cold. But Leicester is the leader of the Puritan party, and the Puritans are panic-stricken at the danger. All the old hatred of the French " Monsieurs Youths " blazes out; contempt for their effeminate gallantry, for their subtlety, for their skill in making love. But Elizabeth, strange compound of statecraft, cunning, and mere woman, is happy. She adds the ape and the frog to the " number of her beasts," and they carry the affectation much farther. The court circle is made up of lions, apes, frogs, partridges, dromedaries, and all the rest of Æsop.

Near this charmed circle of the English Circe, but not yet of it, emboldened by the favor of the great earl and his brilliant nephew, ambitious to be a man of consequence, stands the youthful author of the *Shepheards Calender*. He is a disciple of Chaucer. Like Wyatt with his fable of town and country mice, also told in Chaucerian fashion, the new poet has in mind a tale of a fox and an ape. Perhaps it is already written in part when in this crisis it occurs to him to treat in allegorical fashion this Æsopian court, in order to show the danger threatening the Queen and his patron. *Mother Hubberds Tale* is the result.

III

The facts are these: *Mother Hubberds Tale* was published in 1591, but the dedication states that it had been " long sithens composed in the raw conceipt " of youth. There is evidence that Spenser got into trouble about it, and that it was " called in." But in 1591 it appeared in the volume of " Complaints," and there is no indication that this volume was criticized. The water must, therefore, have become lukewarm by 1591. It seems to me possible to show now just what its temperature was when the poem first saw the light.

The conventional view is that Spenser's trouble arose from the fact that he attacked Burghley, and that the reason for this attack lay in Burghley's failure to appreciate the talents of the young poet. But a moment's consideration must show the absurdity of this view. Can we conceive that a young and ambitious man, no matter if disappointed over some prospective position, would vent his feelings by writing a vitriolic attack upon a man so powerful as Burghley? He may have done so in 1591; indeed the picture was in all probability retouched at that time. But the man who wrote so cautiously about offending great personages as Spenser did in his letter of October fifth to Harvey, would not have committed suicide by such an attack on Burghley in 1579, unless he had some other motive than disappointed ambition, or was playing for a greater stake. We must, therefore, either suppose that in its first form the *Tale* was a harmless adaptation of Renardic material, afterwards retouched into a severe attack upon Burghley, or that there were things in the early version which cost Spenser dear. The first of these views is untenable, for the trouble antedated 1591. It is needful to ascertain just what there was, in the first draft, to give offence.

The two main incidents in *Mother Hubberds Tale* constitute an allegory of the court in which the courtiers are animals. The relation between these two passages is somewhat perplexing. In the first, the fox and the ape, having tried various employments without success, meet the mule, and are directed by him to the Court, where, they are told, they will reap a rich reward if they follow a crafty course. They take the mule's advice, and the ape assumes the airs of " some great Magnifico," and " boldlie doth amongst the boldest go." Reynold, his man, spreads the impression that his master is a powerful lord, and for a time they have everything

their own way. Incidentally we have *a*) the reference to Leicester's marriage; *b*) the description of the
perfect courtier; *c*) the description of the foreign
adventurer and his false arts; *d*) the bitter passage on
suitors' delays. At length they are discovered, and are
compelled to quit the Court. In the second episode,
which immediately follows, we are told that after long
wandering they come to the forest where the lion lies
sleeping, his crown and sceptre beside him. The ape is
afraid, and turns to flee, but the fox tells him that here
is the chance of their lives. " Scarce could the ape yet
speake, so did he quake "; but he asks the fox to explain himself. After a prolonged debate, the ape agrees
to assume the sceptre, " yet faintly goes into his worke
to enter," being " afraid of everie leafe." He goes on
tiptoe, but he is " stryfull and ambicious," while the fox
is " guilefull, and most covetous." The fox agrees that
the ape shall be king, " Upon condition, that ye ruled
bee In all affaires, and counselled by mee." Then they
proceed to the Court. There is significance in the statement that the ape-king protected himself by appointing
" a warlike equipage Of forreine beasts, not in the forest bred." The fox enlarged his private treasures, kept
charge of all the offices and leases, sold justice; he fed
his cubs " with fat of all the soyle," and loaded them
with lordships; he violated all laws, " though not with
violence "; his " cloke was care of thrift, and husbandry." So they ruled, till one day high Jove saw, and
sent the son of Maia to awaken the rightful sovereign

from sleep. The lion rushed to the Court, slew " those warders strange," tried the fox, but let him go free, and ordered that the ape should lose his tail and half his ears.

That the second of these episodes is clearly an after-thought, and not a part of the original plan is, I think, evident. In the first place, the second story is not characteristic of those forms of the Renard cycle which Spenser seems to have used. Again, the two courts are not the same, nor is the allegory. The first story is a general satire on court life, such as we find in Wyatt, and frequently in sixteenth-century literature in England and on the continent. The theme is at base a familiar incident in the Renard stories, with certain conventional Renaissance accretions, such as the contrast between the noble courtier and the base, and the satire on suitors' delays. Very probably this passage was retouched *ca.* 1591, after Spenser had had an experience he surely could not have met in 1579; but this has nothing to do with the fundamental relationship between the two stories. The second incident, on the other hand, is more specific; the allegory is the prominent element; the conception of a court of beasts is stressed; the general satire less evident. Moreover, the characterization is utterly different. Passing by the fact that the lion in the first incident is a courtier, in the second the king, we find that the ape is not the same in the two stories. In the first, he is bold and confident; in the second, he is weak, cowardly, completely the tool of the powerful fox. To this point, which is important, add that the ape-king protects himself by a guard of " foreign " beasts, and the conclusion is irresistible.

In the second story the ape is Simier, or possibly Simier plus Alençon; the fox is Burghley; the lion, or sovereign, is Elizabeth. The purpose of the allegory is to show how a combination between Burghley and the French favorites threatens the Queen, who is unconscious of her peril. If the combination succeeds, Burghley, the fox, will really rule the weak king-consort who has no right to the throne, and who surrounds himself with Frenchmen, foreign beasts, while he and the fox plunder the country, subvert religion, virtually depose the rightful sovereign, and despoil the native beasts.

Reviewing the main points in the argument, we have seen that Burghley and Leicester, rivals always, have special interest in this marriage; Burghley being popularly credited with favoring the match, employing fox-like methods, seemingly innocent and caring only for " thrift " and " husbandry," while in reality seeking to make himself powerful at the expense of Leicester. We have seen that the Queen in the winter of 1579-80 was blind to what the Puritans regarded as a national peril, being completely infatuated with her dissolute and effeminate admirers. We have seen that there was a wide-spread fiction making the courtiers animals and the court an assembly of beasts,—a beast-fable in application, appealing to the Elizabethan fondness for such allegories. With all this Spenser was familiar at first hand. He was in the service of Leicester, and at the very time of the crisis, in early October, was expecting to be sent on a mission for him. His patron, therefore, who had everything to lose by this marriage, since Burghley and not Leicester would rule the French favorites, should be warned of the danger; perhaps the Queen herself should be warned. So Spenser takes his imitation of Chaucer, written perhaps not long before, applies the beast-allegory to the crisis among Elizabeth's beasts, and with a daring not less great than Sidney's own, speaks his mind. Here we have reason for the traditional enmity of Burghley; we have also reason for Spenser's being shipped to Ireland the following summer; we have the grounds on which the poem was " called in." Spenser was ambitious to succeed as Sidney was succeeding; his literary talents were to be a means for advancing him in the service of the powerful earl; at the same time he spoke sincerely the astonishment and terror of Englishmen at the imminence of the monstrous foreign alliance, to the dangers of which the Queen seemed through her passion utterly blind.

More subtle than the vigorous denunciations of Stubbs and the Puritan pulpits, *Mother Hubberds Tale* is not less daring. If it lacks the manly frankness of Sidney's famous letter, it has the same aim. Perhaps Spenser's motive was less pure, for he wished to serve Leicester and thereby advance himself; but there is no harm in a young man's seeking preferment through making himself honorably useful; and the ring of conviction, the sureness of touch which makes this satire a masterpiece, is proof of sincerity. Spenser allowed the caution revealed in his October letter to be overcome by the crisis. The whole episode has that touch of the dramatic so characteristic of the times, not less interesting in that Spenser was not to be one of those who had prominent places among the *dramatis personæ*. It meant success, or exile: he played for a high stake, and he lost.

Some minor pieces of evidence deepen the impression that the *Tale* belongs to the year 1579-80. One of these is the prevalence of the Plague in both France and England during that period, and it will be remembered that the *Tale* makes reference to such a visitation. Again, the entire poem reflects the hatred of French gallantry and intrigue especially characteristic of these years. Simier is said to have turned the Queen's thoughts aside from topics that might awaken her ambition, " disposing her to listen rather to tales of gallantry and such conversation as might engage her affections." The character of Alençon, as summarized by his sister, is precisely that of the ape; " if fraud and infidelity had been banished from the earth, there was in him a stock sufficient of both from which it might have been replenished." In her Progress of 1578, the Queen was attended by a number of young Frenchmen, whom the English called in derision " Monsieurs Youths." All this is reflected in Spenser's poem. Finally, direct evidence is supplied by the well-known reference to

Leicester's marriage ("but his late chayne his Liege unmeete esteemeth," etc.), which would lose its point had it not been written soon after Simier revealed the fact of this marriage, in 1579. The allusion is capitally adapted to a poem designed to rouse the earl to greater zeal in opposing the wiles of the ape who had got him into such trouble.

With the later history of *Mother Hubberds Tale* we are not now concerned. It is worth noting, however, that when it was published in the volume of *Complaints* (1591), Burghley was very unpopular. The quarrels between the Puritans and the Catholics, the growing infirmities of age, the war with Essex over the appointment of Sir Robert Cecil to the Privy Council and later to the secretaryship left vacant by Walsingham's death, and the growing influence of Raleigh with the Queen, are examples of the troubles he met. Spenser was intimate with both Essex and Raleigh, and had been disappointed of advancement; the complimentary sonnet prefixed to the *Faerie Queene* in 1590 had failed to bring results. The *Tale,* as revised, reflects some of the poet's new resentment, as in the passage wherein the fox is made to prefer his own cubs for important offices, a palpable reference to the quarrel over Sir Robert's advancement. Another allusion to the same quarrel with Essex and Raleigh is in the *Ruines of Time.* In 1592 a deposition was made in which it was said that "England was governed by the Machiavellian policy of those who would be kings and whom it is time were cut off."

Trouble arose over the discovery that Burghley had farmed the customs; and frequent complaints against him were lodged with the Queen. Thus we can understand how Spenser's own disappointed hopes, together with Burghley's troubles with Essex and Raleigh and the criticism directed against him from other sources, should give point to a revised edition of the *Tale* in 1591. In 1579, however, Spenser's attack was not personal; it reflected the popular idea that Burghley was favoring the French marriage in order that he might himself increase his power and ruin Leicester; Spenser was in the employ of the earl and sought to do him service. Perhaps he even feared that Leicester would be blinded to the consequences of the alliance.

The significance of *Mother Hubberds Tale,* therefore, proceeds 1) from the fact that Spenser was elated because of his new intimacy with Leicester, Sidney, and Dyer, and his evident purpose to be a man of action as well as a poet; 2) from the fact that the Queen's court was regarded as an assembly of beasts, each courtier being given a name as in the Renard cycle of tales; 3) from the fact that fox and ape, Burghley and Simier and Alençon, seemed on the point of succeeding in their supposed attempt to gain control, this being possible because of the blindness of the Queen through her infatuation; and 4) from Spenser's attempt to second Sidney and other Puritans in voicing the horror of the people and warning Leicester, as the head of the Puritan party, to prevent the alliance from being consummated. For such a purpose the allegory was admirably suited. It is not necessary to consider the poem as a whole to have been written with this purpose in view. The indications are to the contrary. The presence of two episodes dealing with court life, different, even contradictory in part, gives reason to suppose that the allegory of the usurpation was an afterthought. It is this that refers to the Alençon intrigue. But even if the poem was written at one time, no one who is familiar with Spenser's methods in allegory will be troubled by the fact that the earlier incidents in the story do not refer to this intrigue; such changes and additions are common in the *Faerie Queene*. The *Tale* is primarily a Chaucerian story based on the Renard cycle, with modifications frequently met in the literature of the Renaissance. But the story of the usurpation, the satire on gallantry, and the reference to Leicester's marriage, these have to do with the intrigue that stirred England to the depths in 1579-80, and these fix the date of the *Tale*.

IV

We have now to consider the consequences of Spenser's daring. It should be remembered that in this year the Queen was for the first time personally unpopular. The marriage negotiations called forth protests that were so bold as to be dangerous. I have referred to the book by Stubbs and to his punishment. In the *State Papers* is a circular from the Council to the Bishops, dated October 5, 1579,—the date of Spenser's letter,

and the time when the Council was holding daily ses-
sions to consider the marriage. This circular gave notice
that the seditious suggestions in the book called *The
Gaping Gulph* were without foundation, and that special noted preachers should declare the same to the people. Even more interesting is Sidney's connection with
the affair. His letter was written in January, 1580, and
states his objections to the marriage, mainly on religious
grounds, thus representing the Puritans. We are told
that he was punished for his boldness by several
months' exclusion from the Queen's presence, and letters from his friend Languet seem to fear more severe
penalties. I have no space to tell of the quarrel
between Sidney and Oxford, the sensation of the time.
Oxford was compelled to challenge Sidney, but "her
Majesties Counsell took notice of the differences," and
commanded peace. Oxford, be it remembered, was the
cowardly son-in-law of Burghley. In view of Spenser's
relations with Sidney at this time, the incident is highly
significant; Sidney opposed the marriage, and Oxford
took advantage of his being out of favor with the
Queen to insult him.

Leicester, too, had his troubles. Burghley and Sussex
favored the marriage. There is proof that when, in
1580, Leicester had dealings with Condé, the object being to form a Spanish alliance against France, Burghley
deliberately incited the fiery Sussex to quarrel with Leicester. He wrote that he came upon Condé and the earl
in an important conference with the Queen. Burghley

himself found the door shut against him. The wily Lord Treasurer expressed no personal grievance at the affront, but he knew his man. When the marriage apparently fell through, in 1581, Sussex threw all the blame on Leicester and tried to arouse the anger of the French against him. Walsingham writes of the great quarrel between the two earls, and says that the Queen commanded both to keep their chambers on penalty of commitment. They pretended to be friends, but she kept them waiting for days before they were forgiven. More direct evidence is found in a letter to Burghley of July 20, 1580, in which Leicester complains that he has found less of her Majesty's wonted favors. He gives particulars of his suits to her for more lands, which had been stayed, and he states that the Queen used " very hard terms " to him. He pleads in this letter for a continuance of Burghley's friendship. Interesting further evidence of the methods by which he sought to ingratiate himself with Burghley is found in a letter in which Burghley thanks him for the gift of a fine hound,— " she maketh my huntyng very certen."

Now if we combine with this evidence as to Sidney's connection with the affair during the few months following October, 1579, and Leicester's troubles with the Queen, Burghley, and Sussex, the fact that *Mother Hubberds Tale* was " called in " and that in the next summer Spenser was sent to Ireland, the case seems clear. We may note that in December, 1580, Alençon writes that he has heard that several individuals in court are out of favor because of their disaffection to him, and begs that they may not be ill-used on his account. And there is Hatton's servile letter of September, 1580, in which he tells of receiving the Queen's most gracious letter on his knees, praises the cunning of her style of writing as exceeding all the eloquence of the world, and closes with the comforting assurance that having made long war against love and ambition, it is now more than time to yield. The draft of an Act against slanderous words and rumors against the Queen's Majesty, found early in 1581, indicates the stern measures thought necessary. It would be easy to make the case stronger, but enough has surely been said to prove that Leicester's position in 1580 was particularly critical; that he was made a scape-goat for the failure of the marriage, as well as compelled to suffer the resentment of the Queen. Much of this resentment was due to the activities of Leicester's Puritan allies, among whom was Spenser, and one can hardly doubt that *Mother Hubberds Tale* was one of the slanderous documents to which objection was made.

Thus one realizes that the over-zealous Spenser cannot have been so valued by his patron as he had hoped in the preceding October. Probably no one was more thankful than the earl that in the summer of 1580 Lord Grey was appointed to Ireland, was in need of a secretary, and was willing to take the young poet. Grey was himself *persona non grata*; for he had been suspected of sympathy with the ill-fated Duke of Norfolk. Ire-

land, Brabant, the Low Countries, these were Siberias
to which over-zealous persons might be sent if needful.
Leicester, Raleigh, Grey, even Sidney, were subjected to
this " cooling card "; Spenser was in distinguished company.

V

If this interpretation be accepted, that Leicester, find-
ing himself in a tight place, sacrificed his young admirer
as well as a fine hound to propitiate angry deities, we
can now explain another perplexing problem in Spenser's work. In few passages in the entire body of his
poetry does Spenser speak so bitterly as in the sonnet
addressed to Leicester at the beginning of *Virgils Gnat.*
The lines have a fierce repression that suggests Milton:

> Wrong'd yet not daring to expresse my paine,
> To you (great Lord) the causer of my care,
> In clowdie teares my case I thus complaine
> Unto yourselfe, that onely privie are.

The poem is marked " Long since dedicated to the most
noble and excellent Lord, the Earle of Leicester, late de-
ceased." There can be no doubt that the dedicatory
sonnet was written before the earl's death (1588).
There can also be no doubt that the reference in the
sonnet, as well as the story of the poem itself, is to
Mother Hubberds Tale and to the punishment which
Spenser suffered therefor. It will be remembered that
the gnat (Spenser) does the shepherd (Leicester) a
service by *warning him of the snake* (the Alençon

marriage). He is crushed, and is carried into a " waste wilderness " (Ireland). "Ay me "; he says, " that thankes so much should faile of meede ":

> For that I thee restor'd to life againe . . .
> Where then is now the guerdon of my paine?
> Where the reward of my so piteous deed?
> The praise of pitie vanisht is in vaine,
> And th' antique faith of Justice long agone
> Out of the land is fled away and gone.

More directly he says,

> I saw anothers fate approaching fast,
> And left mine owne his safetie to tender;
> Into the same mishap I now am cast.

Other exiles return, but

> I, poore wretch, am forced to retourne
> To the sad lakes.

Line after line might be quoted to the same effect: the poet, exiled to Ireland because of the service he rendered his patron, complains of the injustice of his hard lot. That service was the warning which *Mother Hubberds Tale* conveyed. Thus we are able not only to explain the sonnet prefixed to *Virgils Gnat* and the allegory of the poem itself, but also to date that poem at least approximately. Spenser wrote it after he had been long enough in Ireland to give up all hope but the hope that Leicester might bring him back. That must have been prior to September, 1585, when Leicester was appointed to the command in the States and got himself into the difficulty from which he was never fully released until his death in 1588. But Spenser, having failed before, dared not send the poem, and it remained in manuscript until, with the first cause, the *Tale* itself, it was printed in the volume of 1591. The two poems, taken together, give the history of that mistake of over-boldness which Spenser wished so pathetically, in his letter to Harvey, to avoid. But the part he played in it all, while an error in judgment, is not discreditable, and his complaint, in *Virgils Gnat,* is dignified and manly.

VI

Several other subjects suggest themselves, among them a reconstruction of the history of Spenser's rela-tions to Burghley. It would have been more politic had Spenser attached himself to the great Lord Treasurer rather than to his rivals. But none understood Burgh-ley, in that day, except Elizabeth. He used men as tools to further his own ends; he played a middle course; fox-like, his strategy seemed insincere and Machiavel-lian. He had attacks of gout or busied himself about other affairs, when exigency required. We can realize, now, that he was not altogether selfish, and that much of his apparent unscrupulousness was due to his desire to attain great ends which could be attained only by unscrupulous means. Leicester was able, but reckless; lacking true patriotism, he was swayed by his passion for the Queen. But he allied himself openly with the Puritans; to them he was a great leader, and he attached to himself by this means such high-souled but impractical men as Sidney and Spenser. Both paid dearly for their connection with the earl. One thing is clear: whatever animosity against Burghley was expressed in the original form of *Mother Hubberds Tale* was due to other than selfish pettishness because Spenser's talents were not appreciated. The idea that at the early time when the *Tale* was first written, and with matters of such weight engaging his attention elsewhere, Burghley was meanly jealous of Spenser because he was brilliant and promising, is too absurd to be longer maintained. Admirers of Spenser's poetry are apt to exaggerate his importance in other respects. Politically he was a very small person indeed; his image of the gnat is pathetically accurate.

The fitting close of this discussion of Spenser's connection with Leicester is found in that later version of the earl's marriage put in the *Faerie Queene*. Belphœbe (Elizabeth) saves Timias (Leicester) but does not realize his love for her. Afterwards, however, she sees him kissing Amoret (The Countess of Essex), and becomes very angry. He pursues her, vainly; goes into retirement; yields to immeasurable grief. The Dove sees him with the ruby and a little golden chain, makes peace between them and they are happy. The allegory does not end in marriage, or in love in the conventional sense; it represents knightly service. Here is a charming picture of the quarrel of 1579, softened by time, and presenting in the happiest light the attachment of the earl for his Queen. One wishes that Leicester might have seen it before the time, four days before he died, when he wrote that message on which Elizabeth penned the words, " His last letter."

In this discussion I have sought to show that it was Spenser's connection with Leicester which caused his exile to Ireland, and that this connection led him to write at least the portion of *Mother Hubberds Tale* which gave such offence, the attack on Burghley being due not to personal grievance, but to Spenser's desire to defend his patron and to aid the Puritans. This has made it possible to offer an explanation of the allegory in the *Tale* and in *Virgils Gnat,* and to suggest dates for these poems. All this throws additional light upon the critical year 1579-80, and a study of the October letter to Harvey confirms the impression that at this time Spenser had plans for his life which, if carried through, would have made serious differences in his later work. For the history of English literature it is highly fortunate that the young poet was not plunged into the maelstrom of political life as were Sidney and Raleigh. Spenser himself was bitterly disappointed; he hoped to be an important figure in his own time. The incident is one of many to prove that the course of a man's life may have a significance quite at variance with his plans for himself.

CHAPTER FOUR

In the preceding chapter it has been my endeavor to show that Spenser, like the other men of the brilliant circle with which he was connected, sought to win glory through political service. At first, he seems to have hoped to take an active part, for he wrote to Harvey in October, 1579, that he was about to be sent abroad in Leicester's service, that he had no time to think on such toys as verses, and that he looked forward to corresponding with Sidney. This hope, however, was soon dispelled, probably because of his speaking too plainly, in *Mother Hubberds Tale,* about the plot to make Alençon the king consort. At about the same time, the *Shepheards Calender* was published, and in it was a carefully constructed and cumulative argument warning Leicester and the Queen that the activities of the papal propaganda in England and Ireland, together with factional troubles in the government, would lead to Catholic supremacy and perhaps the overthrow of Elizabeth. As a result of these publications by a man not yet powerful enough to venture on such boldness, he was shipped to Ireland as secretary to Lord Grey.

Moreover, Spenser was from the first a student of theories of government. Harvey writes: "What though Il Magnifico Segnior Immerito Benivolo hath noted this amongst his politique discourses and matters of state and governmente that the most courageous and valorous minds have evermore bene where was most furniture of eloquence and greatest stoare of notable orators and famous poets," etc., a statement which not only recalls Sidney's theories as to the value of poetry to the state and Spenser's own lost work on the *English Poet,* but also suggests the fact that in the circle in which Spenser moved literature was an avocation, not a trade. Again, in the *Faerie Queene* is found abundant evidence that he carefully studied the chronicles of past history and that he made use of current politics for purpose of his allegory. In the *Veue of the Present State of Ireland* he showed thorough acquaintance with Machiavelli and proved that he understood the real meaning of *Il principe* far better than most of his contemporaries.

There is at first sight nothing remarkable in Spenser's allegorical treatment of national dangers in *Mother Hubberds Tale* and in the *Calender.* Such early dramas as *Gorboduc* and *Kynge Johann* contain similar warnings; Lyly's *Sapho and Phao* is another allegory of the Alençon matter, as is also his *Endimion,* though from a viewpoint hostile to Leicester, as might be expected from a poet whose patrons were Burghley and Oxford. Gascoigne in 1575 wrote a masque for the use of Leicester in entertaining the Queen at Kenilworth, which was designed to further the ambition of the earl to gain her hand. But most examples of this kind of work are isolated, mere attempts to gain the favor of some powerful personage or works written at the behest of some patron. Spenser differed from all other literary men of his time in that he persistently clung to that conception of a poet's function that made him a *vates,* a " seer," a man who should warn and advise, directly or through cloudy allegories, those who ruled England. Every important production of his pen, with the exception of his *Amoretti* and the *Hymnes,* is an illustration of this statement. Moreover, a study of these works in chronological order proves that he was not merely a dreamer, an idle singer in an empty day, a poet's poet, but a farsighted student of government who saw clearly the great destiny of his nation. How this element in his work persists and enlarges it is my purpose in this chapter to point out.

I

What the feelings of Spenser were when he learned that he was to go to Ireland instead of to the Continent it is impossible to say. He may not have relished the change in plan, though his objection could not have been due to his desire to remain in London. It must be remembered that he belonged to the circle which included Sidney, Raleigh, and Fulke Greville, and that these men were not town gallants but adventurous spirits who despised the vices and effeminacy of the courtier class. There are in Spenser's works, in the *Mother Hubberds Tale,* in *Colin Clout,* in the *Faerie Queene,* too many passages that pour contempt on those who loafed about the court, making a living by their wits, aping the gallantries and affectations of the French and Italians, to make it conceivable that he wished to be of their number. No small part of the task that confronted Elizabeth was the government of restless and eager men like Drake, Gilbert, Raleigh, Sidney, who felt the intoxication of England's dawning greatness and like Tamburlaine sought to add new realms to its domain. In 1576 Gilbert wrote the tract which first suggested the duty of England to seize and colonize the lands across the seas; two years later he received a charter authorizing him to fit out an expedition to carry his project into execution: in 1583 he sailed with five ships to plant a colony in Newfoundland. Raleigh was forbidden to accompany him on this expedition, but in 1584 Virginia was named by him and in the next few years he was ceaselessly employed in furthering the project of colonization. Sidney was sent to the Low Countries to prevent him from carrying out his project to curb the power of Spain through naval attacks and colonization; the testimony of Fulke Greville shows how persistently he warned Elizabeth of the danger from Philip and how earnest he was in urging his plan of defense and counter attack. Greville records his own dissatisfaction at being kept at court by the Queen and tells how he ran away repeatedly, only to be denied the gracious presence for months at a time when he crept back. When, therefore, Spenser, alert, young, eager, realized that his stay in Ireland meant that he was to be cut off from participation in these stirring projects, the revulsion of feeling, at first intense and terrible, found expression in his splendid protest to Leicester in *Virgils Gnat:*

> Wrong'd yet not daring to express my paine,
>   To you (great Lord) the causer of my care,
> In clowdie teares my case I thus complaine
>   Unto yourselfe, that onely privie are.

But this mood, I am convinced, was temporary. Those biographers who represent Spenser as the poet of ideal beauty whose own life was disfigured by moroseness, who see in all his later work only the vain attempts of an imprisoned bird to regain its liberty, who regard him as a servile functionary ready to give literary sanction to barbarous and inhuman practices, snarling at the estate of poets, satirizing the vices and manifold corruption of court while doing everything in his power to gain a recall, are surely unjust. The warrant for such views apparently given by the *Teares of the Muses* is inapplicable, for this poem is incontestably early work and represents such conventional complaints as can be duplicated scores of times in the literature of the sixteenth century. The references, scattered through the *Faerie Queene,* to the wild and savage country in which he was compelled to do his work are more serious, but they too reflect mainly the conventional protestations by the poets of the meanness of their verses. The later books of the epic, particularly the fourth and the sixth, indicate peace and content, not moroseness or wild despair. The tract on Ireland cannot be defended as a work of pure literature, yet it has its merits notwithstanding, while the positive evidence of *Colin Clout* proves contentment with his lot rather than bitter disappointment, and the fifth book of the *Faerie Queene* shows the poet's art at its zenith. Spenser was not to be sent as ambassador on affairs of state, he was not to be associated with his friends in the great projects that made the air electric, but he was to be the laureate of the new England, defending that national policy which, however cruel and narrow in some of its applications, was to enable her to thwart the foes that threatened her destruction.

Like all sustained poems, the *Faerie Queene* suffers from its length. One reads the first book, notes the form of its stanza, the beauty of its descriptions, the liquid melody of its verse, perhaps the intricacy of its allegory. But the poem lacks the variety of the *Canterbury Tales* and the effect of unity given the separate stories in the *Idylls of the King*. Even *Paradise Lost* possesses the advantage of presenting its most interesting and thrilling narrative in the first two books, while Spenser's poem seems academic, and the triple allegory, even though one try to follow Lowell's advice, persistently intrudes. This is partly due to the fact that at least the first book represents early work, when the complicated allegory was the poet's chief object; it therefore suffers not only from the fact that allegory does not appeal to our naturalistic age but also because it has not

the simplicity and directness of Bunyan or of Tennyson.
It is in the last three books that we find a revelation of
the mature thought of the poet that holds the attention.
The fourth book is a complete exposition of his theory
of love, supplementing admirably the *Fowre Hymnes;*
in the fifth is presented his theory of the state, and in
this his mastery of the allegory is complete; while the
sixth develops from all points of view a theme that
runs through all his works, the praise of the simplicity
and sincerity of life away from the heated atmosphere
of the court, and indicates at least an intellectual recon-
ciliation with his environment.

In the fifth book we have no longer the personified
virtues and vices of mediaeval allegory, everything
being subordinated to the treatment of problems of government. The book as a whole bears on the three cru-
cial events in the reign of Elizabeth prior to the collision
with Spain in 1588: the suppression of the rebellion in
Ireland, fomented as it was by the policy of Philip; the
trial and execution of Mary, also a necessary step in
repelling Spanish aggression; and the direct attack on
Spain through intervention in the Netherlands. The
theme of the book is the necessity for the exercise of
imperial power to the utmost in putting down rebellion
active and incipient, the right of a strong nation to aid
an oppressed and suffering people, and, in some minor
passages, the right of England to establish an empire
beyond the seas. The method of the book is to tell, by
means of incidents suitable to a metrical romance, the

story of Grey's experience in Ireland; to present from two points of view a defense of Elizabeth's execution of her rival; and to relate the experience of Leicester in the Low Countries. But deeper than this allegorical treatment of contemporary events lies the exposition of a theory of government that makes the book one of the most remarkable productions of its time.

The greatest space is given to the Irish problem. Irena (Ireland) must be delivered from Grantorto (Spain) by that queen whose glory it was to aid all suppliants and to be the patron of all weak princes (i, 4). Artegall, who represents Justice united with sovereign Power, on this occasion personified by Lord Grey, is deputed for the task. Then follows a series of incidents by which Spenser gives a vivid picture of the wretchedness of the country. The Squire mourning over the headless trunk of his love is a symbol of the woe wrought by murder and lawlessness (i, 13-30). The story of the Saracen and his daughter Munera (ii, 1-28) illustrates the evil of bribery and corruption in government. How directly this applied is revealed not only in Spenser's prose tract but in many of the letters and documents of the period. In the larger conception of the problem of government, it represents something more serious than lawlessness. Braggadocchio, who claims the victory really won by Artegall (iii, 14, 15; 20-22) represents those who by defamation of others and by self-seeking aim at securing credit not rightfully theirs. Here the historical reference seems to be to the

quarrels among the English leaders in 1580; they plotted against each other, sought to thwart all plans for
progress, and sent to England letters filled with petty
jealousy and malice. The larger significance of the
story, including the account of the way in which all the
people and even the knights themselves were unable to
distinguish between the true Florimel and the false, is
to show the danger to the government from men who
are selfish and unscrupulous, a danger increased from
the fact that the crowd does not accurately judge
between merit and pretense. To enforce this distrust of
the crowd (*vulgus*), Spenser introduces by way of
parenthesis or interlude the story of the giant with
scales (ii, 30 ff.), showing that socialistic theories of
property and democracy are vain.

Spenser now discusses the paramount right of the sovereign over all subjects (cantos iv ff.). The historical
material is drawn from the events in the north from the
uprising of the earls to the execution of Mary. The incident of the two brothers who quarrel over the treasure
chest cast on the shore by the waves is somewhat
obscure (iv, 4-20). At first sight, it is but another of
the minor incidents scattered through the book to illustrate the simplicity of justice; other examples being the
interesting modification of the judgment of Solomon,
where Artegall discerns which of two knights truly
loves a woman by proposing to cut her in half and give
each a portion (i, 25, 26); the decision as to the true
and the false Florimel (iii, 22-24); and the awarding

of the horse to Guyon (iii, 35). But the incident is apparently founded on fact, since it refers, I believe, to the story of Northumberland's claim of treasure cast ashore in his jurisdiction in 1560, and possibly also to his claiming of the custody of Mary on the ground that she had landed in his territory. In 1566 Parliament refused to sanction the Queen's claim to minerals wherever they might be found, thus recognizing Northumberland's objection to the attempt of the Queen to mine copper at Keswick. Spenser probably means to assert the right of the Queen to lands, leavings of the sea, which had been discovered by her mariners, and the passage should be compared with his defense of Raleigh's projected expedition to Guiana (IV, xi, 22) and with the references, in *Colin Clout,* to Elizabeth as the Queen and to Raleigh as the Shepherd of the Ocean.

In the episode of Radigund, the great rebellion of the earls is again made use of, this time through the fact that Grey was concerned in it in some degree. Apparently Spenser attributes Grey's sympathy for Mary to the influence on him of her personal beauty (v, 12; vi, 1; viii, 1). By far the most interesting aspect of the case, however, is the application to Ireland. It will be remembered that Artegall, disarmed by the beauty of Radigund, is made to assume the dress of a woman and to perform the menial tasks of a woman (v, 23-25; vii, 37-41). With this should be compared the sad state of Turpine, found by Artegall in the power of women, his hands tied behind his back (iv, 22). Here we have an arraignment of womanish methods applied to the solution of the Irish problem; Artegall clad in woman's garments and with a distaff in his hand is a fit representative, says Spenser, of the course advised by some.

The story of Samient (viii) introduces more specifically the attempts of Philip to undermine the power of Elizabeth. She represents Ireland, and serves Mercilla, who represents Elizabeth's gentleness and mercy as Britomart represents her might. Mercilla is in danger from the machinations of a mighty man

> That with most fell despight and deadly hate
> Seekes to subvert her crowne and dignity,
> And all his powers doth thereunto apply.
>
> .   .   .   .
>
> Ne him sufficeth all the wrong and ill
> Which he unto her people does each day;
> But that he seekes by traytous traines to spill
> Her person, and her sacred selfe to slay;
> That, O ye Heavens, defend! and turne away
> From her unto the miscreant himselfe;
> That neither hath religion nor fay,
> But makes his God of his ungodly pelfe,
> And idols serves: so let his Idols serve the Elfe!
>
> [Stanzas 19, 20.]

Here is a pretty accurate picture of Philip: his secret plotting against England; his trust in his riches, an allusion to the vast stores of gold secured from the American voyages; his idolatry. The Saracens sent to destroy Samient represent the Spanish expeditions designed to wrest Ireland from England, one of which Grey de-

stroyed at Smerwick. The triumph of Arthur over the
Soldan prophesies the end of Philip.

The allegory is continued in the next canto in the
account of the capture of Guile, described like one of
the wretched outcasts that continually warred on the
English in Ireland (ix, 8-11); his den, his flight, his
many changes of form (ix, 12-19) give a vivid picture
of the difficulties encountered by those who tried to
stamp out the rebellion of the natives. It is noticeable
that neither here nor in the story of Irena, nor, indeed,
in any of the tracts dealing with the subject do we find
Ireland identified with these outcast natives. To Spenser
and his contemporaries Ireland is the fair realm to be
made fit for habitation as a part of the English domain;
the " wild Irish " do not enter into the calculation
except as they may benefit by the peace that is to follow
the subjugation of the rebellious chiefs and the casting-
out of Spain. But in England itself would the lower
classes have received a whit the more consideration in
Spenser's time? And what of Fielding's and Gold-
smith's accounts of the miseries of the poor and the
injustice which they found in the courts and prisons of
the eighteenth century? And Dickens? Why pour vials
of wrath on Spenser's head for not being two or three
centuries in advance of his time in respect to the doctrine of the equality of men?

The object of this lengthy analysis of the political
allegory in the fifth book has been to show how admir-
able is Spenser's method and how complete his interpre-

tation of contemporary history. The remaining cantos, dealing for the most part with the execution of Mary and the intervention in the Netherlands, require no special treatment; their excellence is apparent to any reader. There is, for example, the brilliant apology for the execution of Mary. In the seventh canto, Britomart, representing Elizabeth as the sovereign power of the nation, slays Radigund (Mary the seducer) without compunction; in the ninth, Mercilla, queenly but gentle and merciful, reluctantly passes judgment upon Duessa. Again, Prince Arthur, personifying the nation as distinct from the sovereign power, is at first inclined in Mary's favor, but is convinced by the evidence against her that no other course is possible. Artegall is no longer Lord Grey, but the Justice and Power that accompany sovereignty, unswayed by prejudice, and really sentences Duessa to death, because Mercilla

> Though plaine she saw, by all that she did heare,
> That she of death was guiltie found by right,
> Yet would not let just vengeance on her light:
> But rather let, instead thereof, to fall
> Few perling drops from her faire lampes of light;
> The which she covering with her purple pall
> Would have the passion hid, and up arose withall.

The Legend of Justice is a charming romance, and its moral allegory, less academic and symmetrical than that of the first book, answers to the fondness of the Renaissance for the epic of the perfect man. But it is much more. The most important events in the history of

Elizabeth's development of a powerful government are treated, not baldly and incoherently as in the chronicles, but in an allegory that unifies and interprets. It is not of our modern type of philosophical history any more than it is modern chronicle, but it illustrates in a high degree that Renaissance tendency to interpret life by means of symbols so apparent in their sonnet, pastoral, novel, and epic. Finally, it passes a higher interest even than these. The Renaissance created the State; it also produced many treatises on the theory of the State. In England this new interest was manifested not only in such books as *Utopia* or the *Boke of the Governour,* or in the translations of Machiavelli and collections of similar political axioms, but also in romances like *Arcadia* and the fifth book of the *Faerie Queene.* Fulke Greville says of Sidney's purpose in writing his novel: " In all these creatures of his making his intent and scope was to turn the barren Philosophy precepts into pregnant Images of life . . . lively to represent the growth, state, and declination of Princes." This comes very near anticipating Bolingbrooke's famous saying, " History is Philosophy teaching by example," and both these aphorisms apply with surprising accuracy to this Legend of Justice. The whole book treats of the danger to England from Spanish aggression; of the need of centralization of power in the sovereign coupled with the inflexible manifestation of that power in dealing with plot and rebellion; and of the right of the Queen to rule the seas and to interfere in behalf of the oppressed people of the Netherlands. Each minor adventure leads toward the climax in the triumph of authority, showing how lawlessness, bribery, selfish quarreling and jealousy among the leaders, the danger from womanish theories of mildness, all contribute to thwart the purposes of the ministers of the sovereign. The story of Ireland's thraldom is twice told, in the accounts of Samient and of Irena; the might of the Queen and the awakened spirit of England combine to free her. Again, the story of Mary's fall is twice told, with consummate skill in its representation of Elizabeth as the personification of English sovereignty and in that other trial scene wherein Elizabeth the woman weeps that she must doom a sister to death. The story of the relief of the Netherlands is also presented in two aspects: as another illustration of the all-embracing tyranny of the Spanish monarch, and as a proof of the dawning sense in the English nation of the duty to aid a weaker people in distress. At the end of the book, in the story of the hags Detraction and Envy and in the hint of the ravages of the blatant beast of Scandal, the theme descends from lofty philosophy to become intimate and tender in the story of how the faithful servant of the Queen returned unhonored, unthanked, and broken-hearted. Here in truth is a turning of the barren precepts of philosophy into pregnant images of life, a life not merely of men and measures, but also breathing the spirit of the new imperial England.

II

The *Veue of the Present State of Ireland* is the prose counterpart of the discussion of the Irish problem in the *Faerie Queene.* I have shown elsewhere that in the main Spenser follows the theories of Machiavelli as to the subjugation of colonies foreign in language, customs, and religion. The first part of the tract, which arraigns the life and customs of the Irish, is not materially different from other contemporary accounts; it seems to have been based as much on these chronicles as upon personal observation, or else all observers of the time are singularly agreed in their opinions and in their choice of topics. The curious poem by John Derricke, " The Image of Ireland," published in 1581, may have had some influence on Spenser's tract. It is a fanciful description of the Irish girls as sirens and the kerns as satyrs; St. Patrick is blamed for killing the snakes instead of the kerns. There is detailed description of dress and manner, and one point in common with Spenser is the attack on the bards as aiming to incite rebellion by their songs praising the wild deeds of their forefathers. The course of action which Derricke thinks England should take is also as rigorous as that laid down in the *Veue:* " Rigour is meeteth where clemencie availeth not." The poem, which is in exceedingly crabbed verse, is dedicated to Sidney, and Harvey apparently refers to it in a letter to Spenser in which he speaks of " an uncertayne autor in certayn cantons agaynst the

wylde Irishe" who used the same peculiar verse as in
Gorboduc and the *Steel Glas*. Much of the historical
matter in the *Veue* comes from the earlier chronicles:
Giraldus Cambrensis, reprinted by Holinshed with continuations by Hooker, Campion, and Stanihurst. Campion dwells on the manners and superstitions, on the
Brehon laws, on the custom of redeeming crimes by
composition, on the glib, etc., as well as the usual matter about the origin of the people. This history, originally dating from 1571, was continued in Holinshed by
Stanihurst, who wrote an extremely euphuistic dedication to Sir Henry Sidney. There is a dialogue on the
subject of snakes which is thus described: " First therefore thou must understand, that his booke is made in
dialogue wise, a kind of writing as it is used, so commended of the learned. In these dialogs Irenaeus an
Englishman and Critobulus a Germane plaie the parts."
Stanihurst pays much attention to language, saying that
" to this daie, the dregs of the old ancient Chaucer English are kept," which he proceeds to illustrate by some
not very apposite examples. Spenser ridicules Stanihurst's philology, but he himself makes comparisons
between Irish words and some found in Chaucer. Hooker's account approaches Spenser's in that he proposes a
method of dealing with the Irish under the heads
" How or by what manner the land of Ireland is to be
thoroughly conquered " and " How the Irish people
being vanquished are to be governed." He insists on
there being a sufficient force to punish severely all who

rebel and advises the English in time of peace to prepare for war; the people are treacherous and to be
watched, they are " craftie and subtile "; they should be
deprived of arms.

On the whole, a comparison of Spenser's tract with
the contemporary accounts and the chronicles proves
him to have been a careful student of the subject, not
merely a writer who gives impressions of his personal
observations. In none of these parallel documents is
there anything approaching the thoroughness with
which he worked out his plan, subordinating the archae-
ological matter and the " ripping up of auncient histories " to a clear analysis of the crisis presented by the
ascendancy of the O'Neils and the presentation of a
theory of procedure based on an accurate understanding
of *Il principe*. This plan has been harshly criticized for
its cruelty, but a brief statement of the situation in 1595
will show the seriousness of the crisis. Since the recall
of Grey in 1582, Burghley had temporized, chiefly in
order to save expense. Tyrone, while professing great
loyalty, was secretly preparing for revolt. In the early
nineties Fitzwilliam, the lord deputy, became alarmed at
the developments; he was charged with corruption, but
appears to have been a brave man, though no military
strategist. He was succeeded in 1594 by Sir William
Russell and almost at once the great revolt was on.
Tyrone leagued with Spain; Jesuits and seminary priests
swarmed into the country. The resident English army
was made up of men said to be of the type impressed

by Falstaff. Russell's hands were tied by the presence of a special commission. A fiery letter from the Queen complains that the more inclined to mercy she showed herself the more insolent the rebels became; the commission addressed Tyrone as " loving friend " and " our very good lord "; the Queen seemed inclined to trust his profession, though Russell said the only course was to capture him and put him to death. Without going any more fully into the subject it is easy to see that in the conflict of authority and in the difficulties imposed by distance, to say nothing of the rabble soldiery intent only on plunder, things had got to such a pass that it is small wonder that Spenser, a student of affairs for many years, a man thoroughly conversant with the situation and alive to the fatal weakness of the English course for fifteen years of his residence in Ireland, should advise " strong medicine." Frequent changes of administration, each of them rightly interpreted by the Irish chiefs as signs of the incompetence of the government to deal with the situation; equally frequent changes of plan, blowing now hot, now cold, had brought matters to a desperate state. In the mean time the miseries of the poor were increased, the country was not developed though a source of enormous expense to the crown, life for the English " undertakers " was not safe, Spain was more anxious than ever before to profit by English incompetence: surely these considerations ought to prove the wisdom of Spenser's advice.

Spenser recorded his convictions on the subject of

administration in four lines at the beginning of the fourth canto of the Legend of Justice:

> For vaine it is to deeme of things aright,
> And makes wrong doers justice to deride,
> Unlesse it be performed with dreadlesse might;
> For powre is the right hand of Justice truely hight.

These lines are not based on academic theory or poetic dreaming, but on actual experience with English administration in Ireland.

Space does not permit the citation of more than one or two of the numberless illustrations of the state of affairs brought about by the constant changes of policy. Back in the seventies, a letter to Burghley protests against the delay in sending Sir Henry Sidney, who, it had been announced, was to be the new governor: " Surely, my Lord, the daily looking for a change doth great harm, for during this interim is the greatest spoil committed, because all the ill-disposed now rob and steal, hoping that the new Governor will pardon all done before his time. God send us soon a settled Governor, and such a one as is fit for Ireland, not Ireland fit for him." In due course Sidney came, but he had a soldiery whose pay was constantly in arrears, necessitating pillage as a means of existence; he tried a vigorous government at first, and then, when he failed of support from London, extirpation of the peasants; when this failed, he begged to be relieved of duty. Another instance may be cited, this time to prove that the same trouble extended even beyond Spenser's time:

Davies, speaking in 1612 of the failure of England to solve the problem, put the blame on the faint prosecution of the war and the looseness of the civil government, and says that the country " must first be broken by a war before it will be capable of good government: and when it is fully subdued and conquered, if it be not well planted and governed after the conquest, it will eftsoones return to the former barbarism." In his summary of the reasons for the failure he included the charge that the soldiers were " governed with the worst discipline that ever was seen among men of war." Thomas Lee, who wrote in 1594 a long " Declaration of Ireland," refers to one occasion when " the said traytors were entreated to accept of their pardon, and had more bestowed upon them for playing the traytors than they demanded before." He accuses Fitzwilliam of bribetaking and graft, and says that he himself has not had ten crowns of his private pay as a soldier in ten years. Froude sums it up accurately when he says that England failed through inability to persevere in any one course; coercion, followed by impatience with the cost, was succeeded by conciliation, and this by anarchy; then the return to coercion and the whole wearisome course over again.

If it be granted that England could not allow Ireland to become the base of operations from which Philip could move directly against Elizabeth, and if it be granted that the vacillating policy that had been the rule of procedure for many years was preventing real development of the country and was more cruel to the natives than to have the question settled once for all, it is difficult to see wherein Spenser should be censured for the cruelty and barbarousness of his views. The cruelty which he advised was the cruelty of Grant at Richmond and of the English colonial policy in India and of the American subjugation of the Philippines; cruelty indeed, but a cruelty that was the truest kindness if one be disposed to grant the necessity of the subjugation. Moreover, it cannot be denied that the whole problem was partially due to the religious crisis presented by the alliance between Philip and Rome. In the Sepetmber eclogue of the *Calender* Spenser spoke earnestly of the danger in the Jesuit mission just then beginning; the next year saw the realization of his warning. The attack was threefold: active proselyting by the Jesuits in England, where the argument was boldly used that the patriot would consider church above nation; aid given the cause of Mary, with active efforts to free her; and the instigation of rebellion in Ireland, aided by forces sent from Italy and Spain. Campion bears witness to the fury roused in England by this triple campaign, and says it was due to the ill success of England in Ireland, the work of Spain against England, and the mission of the Jesuits. Between 1580 and 1584 repeated efforts to assassinate Elizabeth and put Mary on the throne, instigated as they were by Parsons, Allen, and Mendoza, opened the eyes of the government to the seriousness of the situation; in 1586 the chain of evidence was complete. Allen was made a cardinal in 1587 and Rome promised Philip a million crowns as soon as he landed in England. This was the result of the campaign begun as far back as 1571, when seminary priests, sent by Allen and disguised as mariners and tradesmen, began the work which Spenser had correctly characterized in the *Calender*.

With the suppression of the Jesuit propaganda and the execution of Mary the chief theater for the operations of England's enemies was transferred to Ireland. After the defeat of the Armada, Philip placed his chief reliance on the attacks on English commerce and on stirring up trouble by the aid of Tyrone. He was back of Tyrone in the nineties as he had been back of Desmond in the earlier revolt. In all this history it is surely evident that England was itself in danger; the war was not merely a battle of religious faiths. Of course, Puritanism had been rather closely identified with Ireland for many years: Sidney was praised by Hooker for his devoutness; his " device of government " was characterized by " religion towards God, obedience to the Prince, the peace of the people, and the well-government in all things touching the commonwealth "; in his family he had " dailie exercise of praiers, both earlie and late, morning and evening, neither would he have anie to serve him who was not affected to religion and of an honest conversation. Atheists and Papists he detested, dronkards and adulterers he abhorred, blasphemous and dissolute persons he could not abide." Grey reported his victory at Smerwick: "The Lord of Hosts hath delivered the enemy to us." Hooker's style is strongly biblical: "They [the Irish] doo nothing but imagine mischiefe, and have no delite in anie good thing. They are alwaies working wickedness against the good and such as be quiet in the land. . . . The waies of peace they know not, and in the paths of righteousness they walke not. God is not knowne in their land, neither is his name called rightlie on among them. Their Queene and sovereigne they obeie not, and hir government they allow not; but as much as in them lieth doo resist hir imperiall estate . . . such is the hardness of their heart that with the rod it must still be chastised and subdued." In his summary of his history he names as the special points wherein England has suffered injustice in Ireland the establishment of antiChristian religion, the depriving of her Majesty of her imperial crown of the realm of Ireland, and the interference of Spain. But it cannot be said that Spenser's tract betrays any Puritanical zeal; his arraignment of the wicked and illiterate priests reflects the mood of the earlier eclogues and does not indicate any conception of the war as a holy war; to him Duessa was more the plotter against the Queen than the representative of Antichrist. In fact, Spenser speaks with scorn of the Puritan predilection for plain and bare churches, and, in the *Faerie Queene,* is far from complimentary when he compares the sect to the Crab, who

Backward yode, as bargemen wont to fare
Bending their force contrary to their face,
Like that ungracious crew which faines demurest grace.

The truth of the matter is that the vituperation and
abuse that have been poured forth upon the *Veue* are
based on two misconceptions: it is regarded as an example of religious intolerance, being due to Spenser's
hatred of the Irish because they were Catholics, and it
is read without proper regard to its historical setting.
How far the first is from being just may be seen by any-
one who will take the trouble to read what the author
has to say about religion. His quarrel, he distinctly
says, is not that they are Papists, but that they are such
bad Papists, being " soe blindly and brutishly enformed
(for the most part) as that you woulde rather thinke
them Atheistes or Infidells." " I doe not blame the
christening of them, for to be sealed with the marke of
the Lambe, by what hand soever it be done rightlye, I
hold it a good and gracious work." He blames those
priests who dwell beyond seas with the Queen's pro-
fessed enemies and " converse and are confederate with
other traytors and fugitives which are there abiding."
He protests against the plotting of the emissaries from
Douay and elsewhere, which he says is more openly carried on in Ireland than in England, where stern measures of repression have been taken. As to the second
point, I have tried to show by reference to other tracts
and documents the reality of the danger to the crown
that Spenser repeatedly refers to. He praises Ireland as

being goodly and commodious, but fears lest God has reserved it for some secret scourge which shall by her come into England. His defense of Grey is based on the altogether incontestable ground that the prisoners at Smerwick were not " lawefull eneymes," being sent by enemies of England " into another Princes dominions to war." The common people are not to blame for their course, for they are the tools of the rebel chiefs; Tyrone owes his power to the encouragement received from " the greatest King of Christendome," as well as from the " great fayntness in her Majesties withstanding him." The advice he gives is to send tried soldiers, well paid and well commanded, to capture the rebel chiefs; then to send colonies of Englishmen to settle the country, after scattering the Irish so that they may no longer be subject to the ambitious chiefs or the comfort of Spain; this done, to give the laws and settled policy that will bring peace and prosperity to English and Irish alike. He has no hatred for the country; it is no wild and forbidding place, but rather " a most beautifull and sweet countrey as any is under heaven, seamed throughout with many goodly rivers, replenished with all sortes of fish, most aboundantly sprinckled with many sweet Ilands and goodly lakes, like little Inland Seas, that will carry even ships upon theyr waters, adorned with goodly woodes fitt for building of houses and shippes, soe commodiously, as that yf some princes in the world had them, they would soone hope to be lordes of all the seas, and ere long of all the world." Here speaks the

imperialist, longing to see so fair a land reclaimed to
ancient glory

> When Ireland florished in fame
> Of wealth and goodnesse, far above the rest
> Of all that bear the British Islands name.

III

From her accession to the year 1588 Elizabeth's policy
had of necessity been defensive. With the execution of
Mary, however, and the humbling of Philip's pride, the
party represented by Walsingham, Raleigh, and Drake
became insistent that a bolder national course should be
followed. With the great increase of interest in travel
and the knowledge that rich territories might easily be
brought within British dominion, to say nothing of the
success Philip had attained in making his colonies pay
the expenses of his wars, they found public opinion
gradually coming to their views. But Elizabeth and
Burghley still hesitated. The " forward school " urged
that the victory over the Armada be followed up by
increasing the navy and planting colonies in opposition
to those of Spain. Had this course been followed, England would not have been so handicapped in her later
attempts at colonization, and the terrible expense of the
Irish campaigns of the nineties, due once more to
Philip's plotting, would have been saved. The most
that the Queen would allow, however, was piracy under
government protection; one finds nearly all the projects
presented to the Queen during this period stressing the

possibilities of securing rich booty. Men like Walsingham and Raleigh saw the larger possibilities in founding a new empire beyond seas, but Burghley was not a
statesman of that type. After the death of Burghley, his
son Robert inherited his power and his policies; madly
jealous of Raleigh and Essex, he blocked all plans for
progress.

Throughout the most critical years of this period,
from 1579, when the Alençon marriage was imminent
and the active campaign of Rome and Spain in England,
Scotland, and Ireland was beginning, to 1595, when
Elizabeth, confronted by the results of Spain's plotting
in Ireland and by the fact that her great rival was
stronger than ever on the sea and in the possession of
colonies that were rich sources of supplies, became convinced of the need of a more vigorous policy, the course
of Spenser was absolutely consistent. In the earlier
period he stood with Leicester and Sidney; later he
gave the support of his literary genius to Walsingham
and defended the memory of Grey; in the nineties he
agreed with the colonial policy of Raleigh and Essex. I
am well aware of the danger in thus comparing the
visions of the bard of fairy-land with the deeds of men
who, like him, saw visions of England's destiny but who
risked their lives and fortunes to make these dreams
realities. In the flush of youth, when he was received
into the brilliant circle at Leicester House, I am convinced that Spenser meant to be a man of action as well
as a writer of verse; no doubt in the later years when

far distant from the court he wrote the epic that his
friends were living he often felt the ineffectiveness of
his life. Like Sordello, prevented from being a man of
action, he sought through the imaginative interpretation
of heroic deeds to realize, in some sort, his ideal.
Drake, it has been finely said, was an ocean knight-
errant, smiting and spoiling in knightly fashion and for
a great cause; a scourge of the enemies of his country
and of his faith. And Spenser, looking in his mirror of
Shalott, saw, in reflection it is true, the deeds of these
knights-errant and interpreted them. He who reads the
records in the calendars of state papers, the letters dealing with the crises and the projects of these eventful
years, the journals of returned travelers, can hardly fail
of the impression that most of these men had little conception of the vast significance of their work; intrigue
and chicane in dealing with foreign powers, penurious-
ness and vacillation in dealing with Ireland, greed for
gold in every charter granted Gilbert and Raleigh and
Drake, marked the policy of Burghley. A few men conceived, perhaps prematurely, an England greater than
any continental power, and to these men Spenser gave
his genius and his pen.

Fulke Greville's account of Sidney is less a biography
than a record of conversations. From these we may get
an idea of the topics that were discussed when Spenser
was on intimate terms with his first idol. We are repeatedly told of his sense of the danger from Spain and the
folly of temporizing; he saw that Philip's power rested

largely upon the richness of his mines in America; he advised open attack on Philip himself and indirect attack by fetching away his golden fleece; to him Elizabeth was the Queen of the Seas, and should keep a strong fleet upon her ocean; as a natural consequence, England should herself establish colonies abroad. The revelation which these pages give of a man whose range of thought and knowledge and whose grasp of great problems of government were so remarkable helps to make clear how extraordinary must have been the contagion of his character. Every one of these leading ideas was reflected by Spenser. Every one of them was contrary to the settled policy of Burghley.

Next to Sidney, Raleigh had the greatest influence on Spenser's political opinions. When the company of shepherds asked Colin to tell the subjects of the songs exchanged between him and the Shepherd of the Ocean, he told a modest story of the loves of the Bregog and the Mulla, and then told of his friend's joy at being again in the good graces of that Cynthia who was Queen of the Seas:

> For land and sea my Cynthia doth deserve
> To have in her commandement at hand.

There is no need to outline Raleigh's great achievement, in action and in his writings, toward the making of an imperial Britain; Spenser's name for him, the Shepherd of the Ocean, is at once a stroke of genius and a proof of understanding and sympathy that outweighs any tract

on colonial expansion that the poet could have written.
All these men were students of government. Gilbert
early gave himself to " studies perteining to the state of
government and to navigations." In the *Arcadia* and in
the conversations reported by Greville, Sidney gave
proof of his interest in large problems. In the " Maxims
of State," in which Raleigh summed up his conception
of these same problems, we have a work drawn, like
Spenser's *Veue,* from *Il principe* and laying down
exactly the same principles which Spenser maintained
should govern the course of England with respect to
Ireland.

Besides the references in *Colin Clout,* Spenser gives
other evidences of interest in the English vikings and in
the development of colonies. The eloquent passage in
the *Veue* has already been cited. The allegory of the
two brothers and the dispute about the treasure chest,
with the conclusion that lands set apart from other
lands by the power of the sea belong to him who seizes
them, seems to be a justification for the right of discovery. That Spenser read with interest the accounts of the
journeys to lands formerly unknown is proved by the
stanza about the " hardy enterprize " through which
daily " many great regions are discovered." Moreover,
he saw in his own epic the reflection of the journeys of
these travelers through uncharted seas:

> Like as a ship, that through the Ocean wyde
> Directs her course unto one certaine cost,
> Is met of many a counter winde and tyde,

With which her winged speed is let and crost,
And she herselfe in stormie surges tost;
Yet, making many a borde and many a bay,
Still winneth way, ne hath her compasse lost:
Right so it fares with me in this long way.
Whose course is often stayd, yet never is astray.

In all this mass of literature, written through the fifteen most eventful and critical years of Elizabeth's reign, is revealed a course unswerving as it is lofty. I have elsewhere alluded to the folly of supposing that *Mother Hubberds Tale* was called in because of Burghley's jealousy of a brilliant young poet who dared resent his failure to secure a good appointment. The present study, I think, throws further light on the reasons for Spenser's hatred of the great chancellor. To Spenser, Burghley represented Machiavellism according to Gentillet; the craft and temporizing and deceit of politicians of this school was abhorrent to his high-souled idealism as it was to Sidney's. This hatred was expressed not only in the *Tale* but throughout the *Faerie Queene* and in *Colin Clout*. In a time when references to political subjects were exceedingly dangerous, when certain passages in Holinshed alluding to Ireland were canceled, and when even such a work as Drayton's metrical version of the Psalms was recalled, it required courage of a high order to write as Spenser wrote. Moreover, he did not hesitate to rebuke Burghley in a way impossible of misunderstanding, as the splendid defense of love in the proem to the fourth book of the *Faerie Queene* proves. Artegall's censure of Burbon refers directly, of course, to Henry of Navarre, but it is noticeable that the policy that he censures,

> To temporize is not from truth to swerve,
> Ne for advantage terme to entertaine,

represents also the very element in Burghley's political philosophy that Spenser detested. Even the sonnet addressed to the Lord Treasurer on the publication of the *Faerie Queene* contains no compliment, and is subtly defiant. Spenser's course was consistent and manly; he was not, like Dryden, ready to change his politics and his religion wherever there was hope of personal gain; his attack on Burghley was due to ideals of government and conduct which he held throughout his life, not to wounded self-love.

Taken as a whole, these writings of Spenser's present an interpretation of Elizabethan political idealism without parallel elsewhere. To regard him as a " functionary " of Leicester, of Essex, or of any other man, or to regard him as a morose and disappointed applicant for the favors of the great, is wholly unjust. Those who find in him the master of a sweetly flowing verse that has made him the " Warwick of poets " shall have their reward. But he was more than this. Dreamer of dreams, Galahad of the quest of Beauty, he was also of good right a member of that little group of men who saw beyond the welter of court intrigue and petty politics the glorious vision of an imperial England. He had his limitations, it is true; at first sight he seems to fail to realize the idea of the nation in the larger sense; one does not find in him the passionate love of native land that quivers through the lines attributed by Shakspeare to the dying John of Gaunt. His loyalty is personal; he conceives the State as Machiavelli conceived it; to him the Prince is the State. Yet on the whole, the two great poets who were the glory of Elizabethan England are of one accord. The splendid lines of Faulconbridge defying a conqueror to set foot on British soil breathe the spirit that animates all Spenser's work, and the England of Gaunt's adoration was to the poet of allegory his sovereign lady queen.

COMMENTARY AND BIBLIOGRAPHICAL NOTES

FOR CHAPTER I

Page 1. The quotation is from Spenser's "Letter to Raleigh," published with the *Faerie Queene,* 1590.

Page 2. The first eight books of an early translation of Polydore's history were edited for the Camden Society by Sir Henry Ellis, 1846 (O. S., no. 36). Sir Henry in 1844 had edited three later books for the Camden Society (O. S., no. 29).

Page 4. The difference between Polydore's history and chronicles of the earlier type may be seen in a comparison with Capgrave's (died 1464), which begins with the creation and gives the history of the world, though its title is " Chronicles of England, to the time of Henry III." The years, in the earlier portion of his work, are entered in a series of consecutive columns and he says he leaves a " vellum bare " in the years of which he knows nothing, so that some later investigator may fill in the blank spaces.

The quotations from Polydore are from the Camden Society edition (O. S., no. 36), p. 30. Polydore's statement of the " law incumbent upon an historian " is found on p. 107.

Page 5. The first quotation is from the Camden Society edition, page 29; the second and those following (p. 6) are from pages 121-2 of the same edition.

William of Newburgh's *Historia Rerum Angliorum* (1196-8) relies on Gildas and Bede. Gildas is praised for truthfulness.

Page 7. As Fletcher points out (*Arthurian Material in the Chronicles,* p. 260), there was nothing original about Polydore's attack on Geoffrey's credibility. Fabyan, for example, expresses doubt, and apologizes to the Welshmen for his brevity of treatment. And Rastell, in 1529, says that Geoffrey does not agree with other writers, but says that every man may believe as much as he chooses. Fletcher's account of Polydore is, however, misleading. It is not true that Polydore did not attack Geoffrey by name. Fletcher's remark (p. 260) that he merely followed the lead of Fabyan and did not flatly reject Geoffrey's narrative is also inaccurate, in spite of the acknowledgement that "this seems to be chiefly unwillingness not to speak out too boldly." The passages from Polydore which I have quoted above are themselves sufficient to disprove this view. Polydore indeed summarizes Geoffrey's material, but his whole attitude is contemptuous not only of Arthur but of everything British. It was his manner as much as his matter that gave deadly offence. The statement which Fletcher quotes from Polydore (p. 262) gives a very misleading impression of Polydore's whole position. Fletcher mentions Leland several times but gives no account of him, and his brief references to Warner and Drayton are quite inadequate.

Pages 7-8. Attention has recently been called to the significance of Arthur as a national figure in an article by Professor Gerould entitled "King Arthur and Politics" (*Speculum* 2. 33 ff.). Mr. Gerould is occupied exclusively with the medieval significance of Arthur and does not deal with the recrudescence of Welsh patriotic spirit which followed the accession of the Tudors. He points out that Geoffrey wrote a history of the kings of Britain, not of English kings as William of Malmesbury and Henry of Huntingdon had styled their books; that Geoffrey's theme is the glory and the decadence of Roman and Celtic Britain, and that he wrote thus in order to give his country an heroic background comparable with that of France. Thus Arthur was intended to rival Charlemagne. In the same journal (2. 318) Professor Nitze calls attention to the fact that much of this explanation of Geoffrey's purpose had been made by previous scholars, notably by Foerster, though not with quite the same emphasis upon the political aspects of the case. Geoffrey may have had the double purpose of exalting the Celts in order to conciliate the party in power, and to aid Stephen by his romantic vision of England's past. The discussion is of interest as calling our attention once more to the significance of the Arthurian material from the earliest times, but not even Geoffrey, with all his confidence in the prophecies of Merlin, could have foreseen the extraordinary political influence his material was to have during the Tudor rule. And despite the great literary influence of his book on the cycles of romance, it was to renew its youth, as we shall see, in Spenser and his contemporaries.

Page 8. Mr. C. L. Kingsford's *Prejudice and Promise in XV Century England* was published at Oxford in 1918. The citation is from pp. 2-3. See also Sir John A. Marriott, *English History in Shakespeare* (1918), pp. 12-13.

Page 9. Hall's *Chronicle* was first printed in 1542; first known edition, 1548. I use the reprint published in 1809, and based on the editions of 1548 and 1550. The first quotation is from p. 423; the second from p. 428.

Page 10. We are not concerned here with the original political significance of the Arthur legend, if it had any. Gerould, in the essay already cited, writes of the medieval politics involved. Loomis ("Arthur in Avalon and the Banshee," *Vassar Medieval Studies,* p. 3) refers to the theory that the Avalon story originated in the national aspiration of the Welsh and Cornish people who throughout the Middle Ages dreamed of a deliverer who should free them from the yoke of foreign rule, and cites Bruce, edition *Mort Artu,* p. 298. But Nitze (*Speculum* 2. 317 ff.) holds that the legend is not English and therefore not national in origin. The whole point of the present discussion, however, is that whatever the original significance, there can be no doubt as to the interpretation placed upon the legend after the accession of Henry Tudor.

In regard to Polydore's following of Gildas in his Roman bias, see J. E. Lloyd's *History of Wales* 1. 140.

Pages 10-11. The citation from Gildas is from the translation of James Copner, ed. 1878, pp. 160-2.

Page 11. Both Leland's text and Robinson's translation were edited with Middleton's *Chinon of England* for the *EETS* (vol. 165) by W. E. Mead in 1925. Leland's *Assertio Inclytissimi Arturii* appeared in 1544; Robinson's translation in 1582.

Pages 11-12. The quotations are from Mead's edition, pp. 7-8.

Page 13. One aspect of this historical primitivism is shown by the use of authorities. Polydore, the Italian, depends on Latin sources; the antiquaries prefer British sources. This may be traced throughout the Tudor historical writings.

Page 15. For Henry VII's use of the descent from Arthur, see *Memorials of King Henry the Seventh,* ed.. James Gairdner, 1858, which contains *Bernardi Andreae Vita Henrici VII* and various other documents. Gairdner speaks of the scanty remains of Henry VII and puts great emphasis on the importance of this work as the only contemporary record. André was a sort of poet laureate of Henry, and was commissioned to write this work and others. It is, therefore, of unquestionable authority.

In his Preface, Gairdner refers to two Latin epigrams on the name of Arthur, Prince of Wales. Of these Gairdner remarks (page lx), " It will be seen how Bernard André in the commencement of his work (pages 9-11), evidently not thinking it advisable to say much about Henry's descent from Edward the Third, goes back to his old Welsh ancestry in the times of Cadwalo and Cadwallader, and speaks of his consanguinity to foreign potentates as a subject on which many had already written. It is evident that either from policy or natural inclination Henry loved to hear his ancient pedigree talked about; and the birth and name of prince Arthur afforded an excellent opportunity for the flatteries of the poets. The prophecy that the former prince Arthur would come again is referred to as having been accomplished in the birth of this boy."

He quotes from the poems of John de Giglis (Harl. MS 336, unpublished) as follows (p. lx): "Two epigrams on the name of Arthur, and a genethliacon or birthday ode in his honour, remarkable as illustrating the importance attached to this old British name and the memories connected with it." Then follows the passage I have quoted above, and a quotation from the poem:

Quicunque Arturum vates praedixerat olim
    Venturum reducem, maximus ille fuit.
Consiliis Superum, jamjam cognoscere fas est,
    Affuit; en dictis praestitit ipse fidem.
Arturi rediere boni non nomina tantum,
    Credite, sed redeunt inclyta facta viri.

And, in a note on the same page, he quotes from Petrus Carmelianus, " who uses almost the very same words in one part ":

Arthurus rediit per saecula tanta sepultus,
    Qui regum mundi prima corona fuit.
Ille, licet corpus terris et membra dedisset,
    Vivebat toto semper in orbe tamen.
Arthurum quisquis praedixerat esse secundo
    Venturum, vates maximus ille fuit.

André (pp. 9-11) traces Henry's descent from Brute and goes on:

Atque ut sui genitoris ab antiquis Britannis regibus descensum breviter attingam, Sancti Cadvaladri, cui post longa temporum intervalla idem Henricus legitime successit, et Cadvalonis praefati Cadvaladri genitoris, si pauca de multis illorum praeclarissimis gestis attigero, priores Britonum reges, ne historiae modum excedam, a quibus idem rex originem duxit, praesens in tempus omittam.

He then tells of the last days of Cadwallader, his flight and loss of kingdom, and continues:

Tempore jam ex illo usque ad Henrici Septimi illius legitimi successoris in Angliam adventum Britonum regnum Anglorum saevitia intercalatum est, et Angli regnare coeperunt. Post itaque praedicti Cadvaladri obitum usque ad Henricum Septimum Britonum regno intermisso, Britones vocabulum amiserunt, et Wallenses ab eorum duce Wallone sunt cognominati; quibus Arturus secundus, antenominati regis primo-genitus princeps, cum haec scriberem dominabatur. Angli autem, ut dixi, qui tunc remanserant et peste superfuerant, incolis de Germania ad se vocatis, insulam inter se dividentes dominium ac regnum Britonum postea repulerunt, Angliamque ab Angularibus Saxoniae populis denominaverunt. Hanc jure divino atque humano post tam longa tempora, post tot bella, clades, et interneciones ab Richardo tertio, qui Edwardi Quarti germani sui binos filios, Eduardum scilicet principem, et Richardum ducem Eboraci crudeliter interemit, divina vindicante, volente, juvanteque potentia, tamquam ab hoste trucu-lentissimo liberans, tyrannidem illius, parva manu morte subacto trucidatoque pro meritis Richardo, ab insula profligavit; et regnare coepit post illius necem toti regno commodissimam, anno videlicet millesimo quadringentesimo octogesimo quinto (1485). Et de ipsius clarissimi genitoris sui nobilissima genesi hactenus.

Prince Arthur was born 1486, made Prince of Wales 1489; André's verses " De Arturi principis creatonie " are in Gaird-ner, pp. 44-5:

> . . . Haec est illa dies qua Arturi saecula magni
> Effigiem pueri sub imagine cernere claram
> Nostra queant. . . .

Note that André's history ends with 1497 and the victory over Perkin, though he has some notes for later years; he has nothing about Prince Arthur's marriage.

Thomas Sharp in his " Dissertation on the pageants or dramatic mysteries anciently performed at Coventry " (1825), p. 155, cites pageants in 1498 in honor of Prince Arthur's visit to the city. In these King Arthur appears with the nine worthies and welcomes this young Prince as a comfort to his old age.

The first quotation from Bacon's *History* may be found in his *Works,* ed. Spedding, Ellis, and Heath, 11. 69; the second, 11. 319.

Bacon's remarks on the pageantry at the marriage of Prince Arthur, 1501, call for an examination of the pageants themselves. There are two accounts: one is a MS in the Heralds' College, and the other MS Vit. A XVI. The Heralds' College MS, probably the official account of the reception, marriage, and funeral of Prince Arthur, contains a minute description of the pageants. It is printed in the *Antiquarian Repertory* (2. 248-333), ed. Grose and Astle (1808), and a condensed account is given in Leland's *Collectanea* 5. 352-381. C. L. Kingsford, *Chronicles of London* (pp. 234 ff.), reprints MS Vitellius A XVI, which he holds to be that of an eye-witness. The pageants themselves are said to have been devised by Richard Foxe, Bishop of Winchester (Kingsford, *Chron. Lond.,* p. 332, and cites Chamber's *Med. Stage* 2. 171). I use Kingsford's reprint for the following account, except for a few additions from the Heralds MS as printed in the *Antiquarian Repertory.*

The first pageant was at the Bridge and included two persons, " Saynt Kateryn and Saynt Vrsula, w^t dyvers livyng virgins." Both saints speak; Ursula's speech (p. 236) is of importance:

> Madame Kateryn, because that I and ye
> Be comyn of noble blood of this land,
> Of Lancastre, which is not oonly of Amyte
> The cause but also a ferne band
> Bitwene you and this Realme to stand,
> Nature shall move us to love alwey,
> As two comyn out of one Cuntrey.
> Trouth it is that out of my lignage came
> Arthure, the wise, noble, and vayllant kyng,
> That in this Region was first of his name

And for his strength, honour and all thyng
Mete for his astate, he was resemblyng
Arthure, the noble signe in heven,
Beawtie of the North w^t bright Sterres seven.

Unto the kyng strong, famous, and prudent,
Nere kyn am I and named Vrsula,
By which name I also represent
Another Image called Mynor Vrsa,
That other wise is called Cinosura,
Set fast by Arthur w^t other sterres bright
Gyvyng grete comfort to Travellers by nyght.

As Arthure your Spouse, than the second now
Succedeth the first Arthure in dignite,
So in like wise, Madame Kateryn, you
As second Vrsula shall succede me.

The second pageant, in Gracious Street (pp. 237 ff.), showed
a Castle, painted and gilded in costly fashion. Here is a man,
Policy, who says Vertue and Noblesse are important virtues.
Noblesse in the castle speaks, then Vertue.

The third pageant, in Cornhill (p. 239), is of great importance: " In Cornhill, where was ordeyned a Costlew pagent w^t
a volvell [This word is glossed by Kingsford as ' an astronomical contrivance with revolving circles,' but note Kingsford
does not see the significance of the contrivance] by which the
xij signes moved aboute the zodiack, and the mone shewed her
course of light and dirknesse. And ouer that voluell Sat, in a
stage or pynnacle, Raphaell the Archangell; And under the
voluell vpon a sate sat iij Astates, Alphons, Job, and Boecius,
called Astronomers."

Note that Vertue had told the princess to go on to this
pageant where she would see " Your kynnesmann Kyng
Alphounce, Which of Astronymy was the verrey well, And of
your ffate the disposicion can tell."

So Raphael says that angels are sent by God to guide, and
that he has a special mission. Alphonsus tells of nativity and

promises greatness to her and to Arthur. Job in a curious speech (pp. 242-3) says he will show another astronomy, not of the philosophers, but to know the creator of all things " of nought." Look above all these heavenly bodies used by Alphonsus

> And ye shall fynd a more specyall pleasure
> To know and behold the great lord of nature,
> All myghty god, that creat and wrought
> Arthur, Hesperus and all thyng of nought.

And he continues that it is the " Sune of Justice, the verray Hesperous, the lyon of Juda, that vanquysshed in fight, Rysyng from deth to lif by his own might ":

> This is Arthure, enlumynyng eche coste
> W^t vij bright sterres, vij giftes of the·holy goste.

He goes on that marriage with Arthur is

> ffor concordaunce of the Cardynall vertue
> Of Attemperaunce atwene your spouse and you.

Boethius follows Job; he represents philosophy. Thus the pageant shows astronomy, divinity and philosophy, three of the liberal arts.

The fourth pageant (pp. 244 ff.) is the most important. In Soper Lane was " the iiij pagent, In maner of an heven, wheryn was paynted the xij signes, and ouer theym was Arthure, clene armed, in his Golden Chare. And in the compas of the firmament wer iij yong stripelongs of the age of xij or xiiij yeres, clene armed the which went evir by avice toward the chare of Arthur, but they neuer passed a certeyn height, vnder these iij Childer Sat certeyn personys, among which one representyng the persone of ffroneas [Kingsford says ' this world is not clear'] had the speche folowyng ";

> [Welcome] vnto Britayne!
> The lond of Arthure, youre spouse most bountevous,
> Whose expresse Image and figure certeyn

Ye may behold all armed, not in vayn
Wt corporall Armour only but in like wise
Wt the spirituell Armour of Justice.

Then to the fifth pageant in Chepe, " a right Costlew pagent,
after an heven wt vij Candelstikkes of gold and candelles of
wax on theym brennyng, And a man goodlike appareiled representyng the ffader of heaven." Here also King Henry and
Queen and great estates of realm waited to welcome the
Princess. The speech was in praise of matrimony, ordained of
God, of church, and an injunction to rulers to love God and
his Church.

The sixth pageant was at Little Conduit in Chepe. Prelacy
and Honour spoke. Then she went on to the Bishop at
London's Palace for lodging. All this took place on Friday.
The marriage was Sunday at St. Paul's.

From the Herald's MS we learn of the decoration of the
palace: " In the wallys and siddys of this halle [' the place of
Rychemont '], betwene the wyndowes, be the picturs of the
noble Kings of this realme, in their harnes, and robes of goold;
Brute, Engest, King William Rufus, King Arthur, King Henry,
. . . The wallis of this pleasunt halle are hongid wt riche
clothes of Arras, ther werkys repr[e]sentyng many noble batalls
and seages, as of I l m [Jerusalem], Troye, Albe, and many
other " (*Antiquarian Repertory*, p. 315).

This account of the marriage pageants in 1501 helps to
disprove the idea that in the time of Henry VII little was
made of the connection with Arthur. It is true that the
genealogies apparently omit Arthur as one of Henry's ancestors,
and that these genealogies were official. Professor Parry
suggests that Henry carefully avoided claiming descent from
Arthur, as being out of the regular line, the emphasis in the
official genealogies being on Cadwallader back to Brutus. But
there is evidence (a) of contemporary recognition of the
significance of the name Arthur given to the young prince;

(b) that throughout young Arthur's life this significance was stressed in pageants—at Coventry in 1498, for example; (c) that Henry regarded the Order of the Garter, a great favorite with him, as " the badge and first order of King Arthur," etc. One should also take into account that the prophecies of Cadwallader were stressed even through the Tudor period, and that the essence of this prophecy was the return of the British line in Henry VII after the gap which followed the death of Cadwallader; i. e., it was not so much the idea of Arthur's sleeping, one day to return, as the bridging of the gap made by the expulsion of the Britons. Put in another way, the idea of Arthur as world conqueror, the historical primitivism idea, becomes prominent with Henry VIII, who in all things liked to think of himself as again giving to the world an Arthurian reign; in the earlier period the first thought was naturally on the return of the British line and the descent from Troy. Finally, the marriage pageants clearly show that the Arthur descent was claimed, and we have an official copy of these pageants, showing the great importance of them in the minds of the government.

Again, this account of the pageants gives the source of Bacon's remarks on the matter in his *History*. He could not have got his information from André, the official biographer, for his account stops with the death of Perkin Warbeck, with two additional sections, neither of which treats the events of 1501. Bacon says that in the pageants there was much of Astronomy, and this remark is now explained. He must have been writing directly from the Vitellius MS or from the Herald's MS. Furthermore, Bacon recognizes the significance of the name Arthur given to the young prince: " In honour of the British race, of which himself was." And finally, of the pageants, he remarks: " Whosoever had these toys in compiling, they were not altogether pedantical." This, also, we can now explain.

But the most important observation is on the source of the pageants. It will be observed that the astronomical elements run through four of the six pageants; that these are the important ones, since the second (Vertue and Noblesse) is merely of the kingly virtues and the sixth (Prelacy and Honour) is a sort of conclusion, giving advice on the relation of the throne to the estates.

Furthermore, these astronomical elements, while perhaps suggested by the eminence of Alphonsus, ancestor of the Princess Katherine, are far more significant than a conventional compliment or a use of astrology in casting a nativity. The machinery used will make this clear. Kingsford notes of the fourth pageant (p. 333) that it was built with four pillars supporting Red Dragon, White Hart, Red Lion rampant and White Greyhound. He does not explain this, though the red-white matter is of course a commonplace. There should be two additional notes: first, the Red Dragon is of course a reference to Cadwallader, whose badge Henry used at his landing at Milford. The other animals are also of emblematic value. Second, the use of emblematic or allegorical animals is a well known characteristic of the Grail stories; I shall return to this point in a moment.

Kingsford also gives (p. 333) a note on the machine, based on the Herald's MS but without noting its significance. His account follows: " In the front was a great wheel, ' wonderfully wrought with clouds.' On the top of this wheel was the Father of Heaven, and in its midst the chair for Arthur. The wheel was adorned with figures and badges. On its broad part were 3 armed knights; ' the which, as they wolde, ascended, and torned the wheel very swyftly all the season of the comynge of the Princess.' The pageant was named the Sphere of the Sun, as ' appropriate to the Prynce of Englond, shewyng and declaryng his fatall dispocion and desteny.' " (This is quoted by Kingsford from *Ant. Rep.* 2. 273.)

Now it is clear that the writer from whom Kingsford quotes did not understand the real meaning of the volvell or cosmic wheel. We must turn to Arthurian romance for an explanation. I give two: In *Titurel* (Loomis, *Celtic Myth and Arthurian Romance,* p. 159) we are told that the Grail Temple was round, its dome covered with blue sapphires, with carbuncles that shone like the sun. Golden sun and silver moon were also set in the dome, and *were moved by a hidden mechanism through their courses.* The rest of the Temple was a replica of the earth, etc.

In *Arthur of Little Britain* (Loomis, p. 174), accompanied by Baldwin, Arthur goes to end enchantments of Porte Noire, a miraculous castle given by Queen of Fairy (Proserpina) to Florens, her godchild and replica (cf. Florimel and Amoret), and watched over by Steven, an enchanter, servant of Florens. They fight with 12 knights, watched over by Steven from the wall. Then to the hall, then to a chamber where " was portrayed how God did create sun and the moon, and in the roof were all the seven planets wrought with fine gold and silver, and all the situations of the heavens, wherein were pight many carbuncles and other precious stones." Then follows the account of the marvels of the magic chamber, treated in my study of the Britomart-Amoret enchantment plot (*MLN,* 26. 117-130).

Loomis remarks (pp. 175-6) the survival here of the conception that the Other World is the sky. At any rate it is this conception which seems to lie behind the celestial orbs which deck the roofs of the Grail Temple and of the Porte Noire, and also behind the nocturnal revolutions of Curoi's Castle.

Too, the pageants in honor of Leicester on his landing in the Low Countries, December, 1585, presented " the ninth shew of Arthur of Britaine " (Holinshed 4. 645) : " Over the entrance of the court gate, was placed aloft upon a scaffold, as it had beene in a cloude or skie, Arthur of Britaine, whome they compared to the earle . . ."

Finally, we note the cosmic stage in the Wagner Book (1594) as a survival of the same myth (see my article in *MLN*, 26. 117-130).

I postulate, pending further investigation, that the source of the marriage pageants is *Arthur of Little Britain*, tr. Berners, or a common source; that it was used by the compiler in compliment to the Welsh ancestry of the reigning house; and that it confirms, indirectly, Loomis's theory of Celtic origins of some of the important elements of the Arthurian story.

In the *Somers Tracts* (1. 26 ff.) is a reprint of Vit. XI from the Cotton Library, in which is given a long and romantic account of the arrival of Princess Katherine in England and of her reception. The editor of the *Tracts* remarks (p. 26) that " the subsequent narrative is written in a strange and romantic style, more like that of Amadis de Gaul, than of an official narrative." The account is divided into chapters, with descriptive matter as in the Romances, e. g., " The fourth chapter, of the demeanor of the Kings, and of the Princess, in their first meeting."

Page 16. Holinshed is quoted from the edition of 1807, Book 5, ch. 12.

Page 17. I quote Bale's Commentaries on Leland's " New Year's Gift," cited by L. T. Smith in his edition of Leland's *Itinerary*, p. xii. Bale's distrust of Polydore was not limited to his treatment of the Arthurian matter. In *Kynge Johan* (ed. J. M. Manly, *Specimens of Pre-Shaksperean Drama* 1. 601) Veryte speaks as follows:

> I assure ye, fryndes, lete men wryte what they wyll,
> Kynge Johan was a man both valiaunt and godlye.
> What though Polydorus reporteth hym very yll
> At the suggestyons of the malicyouse clergye,
> Thynke yow a Romane with the Romans can not lye,
> Yes; therfore, Leylonde, out of thy slumbre awake,
> And wytnesse a trewthe for thyne owne contrayes sake!

While this may be a reference to Leland's insanity, it is more probable that the author calls upon him to see a deeper perfidy in Polydorus than mere rejection of British claims. Polydorus is not only the defamer of Britain but the ally of Rome; Leland does not see this more subtle danger and is called from his " slumber."

Among other attacks on Polydore in the sixteenth century we may note the following: Arthur Kelton, *A Chronycle with a Genealogie declaryng that the Brittons and Welshemen are lineallye dyscended from Brute. Newly and very wittely compyled in Meter* (1547). This work, dedicated to Edward VI, traces the British kings from Osiris, " the firste kyng of Egipt," through the Trojans to King Arthur and the Tudors, ending with Edward VI. In the course of the chronicle, he takes a fling at Polydore Vergil:

> But first to you, master Polidorus
> Your conscience, onely to discharge
> Whiche of long tyme, hath been oblivious
> Against vs Brutes, in writyng so large
> Your spirites incensed, all in a rage
> By your reporte, vs to inflame
> Your pen to rashe, your termes out of frame
>
> Where is become, your bounden deutie
> Our antecessours, this to deface
> Sith it pleaseth, the high Maiestie
> Of our most noble, the kynges good grace
> Not to disdaine, as in this case
> To be compted, of the same stocke and lyne
> Doune by dissent, to this present tyme. (sig. E 2 and verso)

After protesting that the British are free from the luxuries and vices of Italy, that

> We Welshemen plaine, that do deny
> Whiche is oft, muche vsed in Italie (sig. E 3)

Kelton adds:

> Withdrawe your pen, Master Polidorus
> Your vain reporte, and fliyng fantasy
> No more in this to amplify
> But what maie stande, with honesty
> Wordes of defame, ye maie well thinke
> Men will requite, euen to the pittes brinke.   (sig. E 3 and verso)

Thomas Twyne, translator: *The Breuiary of Britayne . . . Written in Latin by Humfrey Lhuyd of Denbigh, a Cambre Britayne, and lately Englished by Thomas Twyne, Gentleman* (1573). Among the prefatory matter are verses headed: " Ed. Grant, Scholemaster of Westminster: in comendation of this treatise of Britanie, pende in Latin by Hūfrey Lhuyd, and translated into English, by Tho. Twyne."

> If for to write of *Brutus* broode,
>   eche *Britaynes* brayne be bounde,
> For zeale he owes to country soyle,
>   and eke his natiue grounde:
> Then *Wales* may boast, and iustly ioy,
>   that such a *Britayne* bred,
> Which hath with serious serche of brain
>   and toylyng trauell spred,
> Throughout the coasts of *Britany*,
>   and forrayne countries strange:
> The liuely fame of *Brutus* name,
>   that through the world doth range.
> That long lay hid in dungeons darke,
>   obscurde by tract of time,
> And almost smouldred with the smoke
>   of ignorances crime:
> But now reuiude and polished,
>   by *Lhuyd* his busie brayne:
> And brought to light, & former frame,
>   by his exhausted payne.
> Whose diligence, and iudgement great
>   I can but muse to see,
> That with such skill doth paynt
>   the prayse of *Brute*, and *Britanie*,

That with such loue to countryes soyle
   doth bryng agayne to light:
The shinyng shape, and stately stampe
   of that was darckned quight.
By whose endeuour *Polidore*,
   must now surseace to prate,
To forge, to lie, and to defame,
   kynge BRUTUS worthy state.
By whose great paynes, proude *Hector* Scot,
   must now leaue of to bable,
Such vaunts: as of his Scottish soyle,
   he whilom seemd to fable.
By *Lhuid* their brags be beaten downe,
   their forgyng lies be spide,
And *Britaine* needs must chaleng fame
   that erst it was denide.
Lhuid findeth forth hir former fame,
   and antique names doth tell:
And doth refute their forged lies,
   that did of rancor smell.
Brutes worthy race is blazed here,
   by trumpe of flickering fame:
And *Lhuid,* it is a flowyng flud,
   that hath reuiued the same.
Who though enterred now in earthe
   yet shall he neuer die,
But liue amongs his *Britanists,*
   by this his *Britanie*:
Whose thread of life wold god the *Fates*
   had yet not sought to spoyle:
Then had wee had a larger scope
   of *Brutus* sacred soyle.
Go little volume, go thy wayes,
   by *Lhuid* in Latin pende:
And new attir'd in English weede,
   by *Twyne* that thee doth sende,
To *Brute* his broode: a labour sure
   that well deserueth prayse:
Go shew thy selfe to *Britanists,*
   whose glory thou dost rayse.

Another verse, "in praise of Arthur," by Lodowick Lhuyd says:

> Thy patron grannde, an auncient Sire
> Aeneas Troiane stoute:
> Did never toile on land and Seas,
> as thou hast rangde aboute,
> From mountaines high wher to thy selfe
> alone wast wont to talke.

This is the Lodowick Lloyd who John Lane says was responsible for Spenser's "laureat" funeral (*Triton's Trumpet,* unpublished MS in the B. M., Royal MS 17. B. XV, fol. 175 verso).

Lhuyd has many references to the quarrel and pays his respects to Polydore and Boece in such passages as these:

[Polydore] sought, not only to obscure the glory of the British name, but also to defame the Brutaynes them selves with sclanderous lies. So Boece defames all but "his Scottes."

I beleeve that Brutus came unto Britayne with his traine of Troians, and then tooke upon him the government of the anncient inhabitants, and of his owne men, and thereof were called Brutaynes. (ed. 1729, p. 5)

How much a man without shame, that Polydorus Virgillius is, who doubteth not to affirme, that Claudius Caesar vanquished the Brutaynes without any battaile, and most impudently calleth them dastards, whom Caesar himself, Tacitus, Dion and Herodian: terme by these names, most warlike, cruell, bloudthirstie, impatient both of bondage, and inuries. But an infamous beggage groome, ful fraught with envie, and hatred, what dareth he not do, or say? (p. 15)

John Caius in *De Antiquitate Cantebrigiensis Academiae,* ed. 1574, p. 52 (cited by Fletcher, *Arthurian Materials,* p. 260n), defends Geoffrey against Polydore.

Page 18. Camden's "Preface" is from the *Britannia* (1586), translated by Philemon Holland, 1610.

Page 19. The remarks of the Dean of Wells are from the introductory note to J. Armitage Robinson's *Two Glastonbury Legends,* 1926.

Page 20. St. Albans Chronicle is quoted from Speed, edition of 1650, p. 164.

Pages 21-3. The citations from Camden are from the 1610 edition, pp. 7-8. It may be noted that he goes on to a new examination of the origin, based on the study of etymology. Camden, therefore stands on the border line between the historical primitivists and the philologists. The study of antiquities through etymologies was wide in the Elizabethan period, and may be observed in Spenser.

Speed is cited from the edition of 1650, pp. 170 and 333.

John Harington, the Queen's god-son, recorded his opinion on Merlin and Arthur in the notes to his translation of *Orlando Furioso* (1591). He refers to Camden, but seems to have made an independent investigation. He says:

Concerning the history of this booke [three], it is divers, and therefore I meane to note the principallest of them, as far as my little reading is able to discover: and first for Merlin (called the English Prophet) I know many are hard of beleefe, and thinke it a meere fable that is written both of his birth, of his life, and chiefly of his death: for his birth, indeed I beleeve not that he was gotten by an Incubus, yet the possibility thereof might be proved by discourse, save it were too tedious, and perhaps too full of unmannerly termes for this place: I rather hold with the great clerk Bellarmine (Bellarmin. de Antichristo), that such birth is either impossible, or peculiar to the great Antichrist when he shall come. But concerning his life, that there was such a man, a great counseller to King Arthur, I hold it certaine: that he had a castle in Wiltshire called after him Merlins-burry, (now Marlborrow) it is very likely, the old ruines whereof are yet seene in our highway from Bath to London. Also the great stones of unmeasurable bignesse and number, lie scattered about the place, have given occasion to some to report, and others to beleeve wondrous stratagems wrought by his great skill in Magick, as likewise the great stones at Stonage on Salisbury plaine, which the ignorāt people believe he brought out of Ireland: and indeed the wiser sort can rather marvell at, then tell why or how they were set there. But for the manner of his death, and place of his buriall, it is so diversly written of, and by so sundry countreys challenged, as a man may be bolder to say that all of them are false, then that any of them be true. Some will have him buried in Cornewall, some in Wales (where they say he was borne,) Ariosto by Poeticall licence, makes this tombe for him in France, and the fiction of the tombe is taken of a former fiction in King Arthurs booke, namely, that Merlin being exceedingly in love with the Lady of the Lake (to brag of his cunning) shewed her one day among other devices of his, a tombe that hee had made of sufficient capacity to hold him and his wife, and withall shewed her a charme, which being pronounced in an order that he shewed her, the tombe would close, and never again be opened. She having no minde to him, or rather indeed flatly hating him, grew on the sodaine very gamesome with him, and shewed him some extraordinary kindnesse, and in the end for want of better pastime would needs perswade him to prove if it would hold them both, and so offered her selfe to goe in with him: he suspecting nothing lesse then her malicious purpose, went simply in, and straight shee shut him in with the cover, and bound it so fast with the charme, as it will never more be loosed. . . .

For the Historie of this booke [four], little is to be said of the time of Charles the great, because the booke digresseth to other matters: but whereas mention is made of Calledon forrest in Scotland, and of king Arthur his knights, I thought it not amisse, as in the former booke I told you, what I thought of Merlin that was Arthurs great counseller, so now somewhat to touch, as the space will permit, the reports that are true and probable of king Arthur. It is generally written & beleeved that this Arthur was a notable valiant and religious Prince, and that hee governed this Iland in that rude age with great love of his people, and honour of forraine nations, hee instituted an order of the knights of the round table onely (as it seemes) of some merriment of hunting, or some pleasant exercises. He was himselfe of stature very tall, as appeares by the proportion of him left (as they say here in our countrey of Somerset) in a doore of a Church by the famous Abbey of Glassenbury, in which Abbey his wife Queene Guenever was buried, and within our memory taken up in a coffin, with her body and face in shew plainly to be discerned, save the very tip of her nose, as divers dwelling thereabout have reported. But what manner of death King Arthur himselfe died, it is doubtfull, and that which they report seemes meerly fabulous, namely that he was carried away in a barge from a bridge called Pomperles, neare the said Glassenbury, and so conveyed by unknowne persons, (or by the Ladie of the Lake) with promise to bring him backe againe one day: upon which it seemes the foolish people grounded their vaine saying (King Arthur comes againe).

For my part I confesse my selfe to have bin more inquisitive of such trifles then a wiser man would, and viewing that bridge and all that countrey about Glassenbury, I see good reason to guess, that all that countrie which now we call our moores (and is reduced to profitable and fertill ground) was sometime recovered from the sea, and might be navigable up to Glassenbury in those times: and so I suppose the said King being drowned there by some mishap, and being well beloved of the people, some fained (to content their minds) that he was but gone a little way, and would come again: as the Senate of Rome, having killed Romulus for his tyranny, devised a tale of I know not what ἀποθέοσις to make the people beleeve he was turned to a god. M. Camden (Camden. in Britannia. Somersetshire) the best antiquary of our time, writeth that King Arthurs body was taken up at the foresaid Glassenbury in the time of King Henry the second, which indeed is most credible, as he there proveth. But this I conclude, that this Prince was so worthy a man in his time, as not only true histories have greatly recommended to the posterity, but almost all Poeticall writers that have bin since, have mentioned this famous Prince Arthur of England as a person of whom no notable exploit was incredible. And thus much for King Arthur.

The reference to the poets is especially interesting, for Harington knew Spenser's *Faerie Queene* and used it in his translation. Note that he speaks of *Prince* Arthur as the subject of the poets. Harington's attempt to rationalize the legend shows his desire to believe it.

An unpublished work of John Dee (Cotton MS Vitellius b VII. 3. pp. 248-264) argues that England was entitled to Iceland because it had been conquered by Prince Arthur.

Sir Robert Naunton in his account of Elizabeth in *Fragmenta Regalia* (1641) says (*Somers Tracts*, 1. 251):

Remarkeable it is, considering that violent desertion of the royall house of the Britaines, by the intrusion of the Saxons, and afterwards by the conquest of the Normans, that through vicissitude of times, and after discontinuance almost of a thousand yeares, the scepter should fall againe, and be brought back into the old royall line and the true current of the British blood in the person of her renouned grandfather King Henry VII.

Page 25. The *Mirrour for Magistrates* is quoted from Joseph Haslewood's edition (1815) 1. 7.

Page 26. Professor J. W. Cunliffe's *Early English Classical Tragedies* was published at Oxford, 1912.

Miss Carrie A. Harper's Bryn Mawr Dissertation, *The Sources of the British Chronicle History in Spenser's Faerie Queene,* was published at Philadelphia, 1910.

Page 27. I use the Spenser Society edition of Churchyard. The quotations are from pp. 26, 27, 29-30, and 33-4 in order given.

Page 29. For Warner's *Albions England,* I use A. Chalmers's reprint in volume 4 of his *English Poets* (1810).

Page 31. The citations from Drayton's *Heroical Epistles* are from the Spenser Society edition, no. 45, pp. 34-5; no. 46, p. 46.

The citations from *Polyolbion* are from Chalmers's edition in volume 4 of his collection, pp. 184, 188, 197, 208, 209, 216, 229, 237.

Page 37. Grosart's edition of Robert Chester's *Loves Martyr* appeared in the Publications of the New Shakespere Society, Series 8, no. 2, 1878. His interpretation of the allegory could be proved impossible by internal evidence alone, but Professor Brown, in his *Poems by Sir John Salusbury and Robert Chester,* Bryn Mawr College Monographs, 1913, contents himself with showing that Sir John was opposed to the Essex faction and that therefore a poem obviously written in his honor could have contained no such allegory, and with proposing a different and far more reasonable interpretation. Professor Brown does not discuss the Arthurian matter in the poem, since he holds that it has nothing to do with the allegory.

The authorship and significance of the Arthurian matter are somewhat puzzling. The title page of the 1601 edition contains the statement that the poem proper, the fate of the Phoenix and Turtle, was translated "out of the venerable Italian Torquato Caeliano,"—which, as both Grosart and Brown hold, though for different reasons, is a deliberate mystification. The title page also states that the poem contains "the true legend of famous King Arthur, the last of the nine Worthies, being the first Essay of a new Brytish Poet, collected out of diuerse Authenticall Records." In the 1611 edition the title page is completely transformed. Instead of giving chief place to the Phoenix and Turtle story, or *Love's Martyr,* we now have "the Annals of Great Britain. Or, A Most Excellent Monument, wherein may be seene all the antiquities of this Kingdom, to the satisfaction both of the Universities, or any other places stirred with Emulation of long continuance." Because of similarities in stanza and style, it seems to me that Chester should be credited with the authorship of the poem about Arthur, despite his statement about the "new Brytish poet"; it is also closely related to the body of the poem, even though the method of its inclusion is awkward even for Chester. As I show later, it may have been written much earlier than the Phoenix and Turtle part, and included as a further compliment to Sir John and as a contribution to the attempt to rehabilitate Arthur. When *Love's Martyr* was first published, the allegory seemed of chief interest; by 1611, this interest had disappeared, and the poem apparently survived for the antiquarian learning which it contained. Sir John Salusbury died July 24, 1612.

Pages 37-38. The quotations are from pp. 33, 34-5 (top pagination).

Page 39. The possible relations of Chester and Robinson have some curious interest. To the facts given above to show that Chester used the additional notes which Robinson put into his book after the translation was made (see Meade's edition, *EETS*, 1925, pp. 12-13) add the fact that Chester speaks of Arthur's one hundred and forty knights; Robinson gives their names (p. 149). One queries, also, whether Chester, or some mutual friend, may not have been the " english man " to whom Robinson refers as the possessor of the French book. Chester's statement in the Preface (see edition by Grosart, p. 35) is as follows: " I my selfe have seen imprinted, a french Pamphlet of the armes of king Arthur, and his renowmed valiant Knights, set in colours by the Heraulds of France: which charge of impression would have been too great, otherwise I had inserted them orderly in his Life and Actions." Robinson speaks also of the expense of impressions, in his reference to " a certaine French booke . . . beeing in an english mans handes, I was not so desirous to see it, but he as willingly shewed it & lent it me. There was in it portracted both the severall names, shieldes, and severall armes in colours also depainted of all K. Arthures knights and under every one the commendation due unto him by his chevalrie. Which because the engraving of their armes was very chargeable, . . . I was enforced to content me with this briefe collection," etc. There follows the description of the shield, which, as I have shown above, Chester followed almost literally. The similarity of circumstances and phrasing is striking; besides, why should Chester, if he wrote the chronicle in *Love's Martyr*, speak of the expense of reproduction of heraldic plates, a thing quite desireable for Robinson, who was writing to gain the attention of the Society of Archers?

Page 40. The reference to Henry VII's view of the Order of the Garter is from *CSP, Venetian* 1. no. 790. The description of the entertainment in Calais is from the same, vol. 3, p. 33. The comparison of Henry with Arthur in 1533 can be found in *CSP, Domestic,* 6 (1533). 515.

Page 41. The letter of Eustace Chapuys is from *CSP, Spanish* 4. 26 (part 2, no. 598).

Page 42. Quinn's sonnets are cited from Miss Evelyn May Albright's *Dramatic Publication in England,* p. 151. Quinn's answer to Spenser is not extant. The pageants at Elizabeth's coronation are reprinted by Nichols, *Progresses of Elizabeth* (1823) 1. 38-65. The account of the entertainment at Norwich is in the same source, vol. 2, p. 143. The pageant at Kenilworth is described in Nicholas, *Progresses* 1. 490-2.

Page 44. The Queen's " thrice coming here " is a reference to two former visits in 1565 and 1572.

The Venetian secretary's view of Henry VIII as St. George is from Reyher's *Les Masques Anglais* (Paris, 1909), p. 8. For the mumming shows see the texts of the St. George plays in Manly, *Pre-Shaksperean Drama,* and the discussions in Chambers. Kingsford (*Chron. of London,* p. 200) cites a pageant in Westminster Hall temp. Henry VII (1494), in which is figured St. George and a castle, with twelve lords, knights, and squires as attendants.

Page 45. The quotations from the *Arte of English Poesie* are from Arber's edition, pp. 188 and 192; see also p. 203. The citations from Peele are from *Works,* ed. Bullen, 1. 351 ff., 261 ff., and 343 ff.

Page 46. Ashe's *Elizabetha Triumphans* is reprinted in Nichols's *Progresses* 2. 545-612. Richard Niccols's *England's Eliza* (1610) was printed in pt. 5 of the *Mirrour for Magistrates,* reprinted Haslewood (2, pt. 2, 823 ff.). The quotation from Peele is to be found in *Works,* ed. Bullen, 2. 331-3.

Page 47. *Fuimus Troes: The True Trojans* is cited from Hazlitt's *Old Plays* 12. The quotation is from act 2, sc. 1 (p. 468).

Page 48. Thomas Hughes's *The Misfortunes of Arthur* is from Cunliffe's *Early English Classical Tragedies.* The quotations are from act 2, sc. 1, lines 1-3; 1. 1. 62-6; 5. 2. 14-30.

Page 50.　Fulbecke's lines are from p. 296.

Page 51.　Professor Mead, in his valuable survey of the Arthurian matter in the Elizabethan period (*Chinon of England, EETS,* 1925) follows Fletcher in his statements about the chronicle material; thinks Holinshed's scepticism may have stimulated Robinson's translation of Leland; cites the interest in archery, with Leland's tract, proves the vitality of the tradition in everyday life; but finds little influence of the literary tradition. The best old verse romances, such as *Morte Arthure, Gawain and the Green Knight,* the Elaine material in *Le Morte Arthur,* were "quite certainly not read in the sixteenth century." Malory was several times reprinted; Ascham protested against the romances; they possibly suggested the *Princely Pleasures* of 1575. For this summary see Mead, Intro. pages xxviii-xxxii. Mead agrees with the theory that this neglect of the romance was due to Puritan prejudice, voiced by Ascham. Sir E. K. Chambers, in his recent book, *Arthur of Britain* (Lond., Sidgwick & Jackson, 1927), confines his attention almost exclusively to the earlier period, making no mention of the quarrel except the statement that Polydore's criticism aroused a storm of protest from Leland and others (p. 131). His thesis that Arthur became Anglicized is the direct opposite of my own; I give an abstract of it as a part of the summary of my chapter. Professors Gerould and Nitze, as already stated, confine their attention to the possible political significance of Geoffrey in his own time, not in our period.

Page 58.　[Since Professor Greenlaw had not written his intended analysis of Arthur's part in the *Faerie Queene* before his untimely death, I have thought it well to reprint the following extract from his article of 1918, " Spenser's Fairy Mythology," *SP* 15. 116-121.—R. H.]

Fairies and Britons

The significance of Arthur's vision of the Fairy Queen is that by this device Spenser is able to establish the basis on which his poem rests. The traditional Arthur was a British king about whose birth many mysterious legends clustered, and who, at the end of his life, was received in *Faerie,* after that last great battle in the West, to be healed of his grievous wound by Morgain, or *La Dame du Lac, or by these and other powerful* fays together. After a long sojourn in *Faerie,* he was to come again and rule Britain. This belief is extant in parts of Wales today, as it was in Layamon's time. Lydgate phrases it compactly:

> He [Arthur] is a king y-crowned in Fairye;
> With sceptre and pall, and with his regalty,
> Shall he resort, as lord and soveraigne
> Out of Fairye, and reigne in Britaine. (*Falls of Princes* 8. 24.)

Spenser's use of this tradition about the fairy sovereign gives the clue to the idea on which the entire poem rests. The interpretation is to be found in the return, through the Welsh house of Tudor, of the old British line to the throne of England, now long occupied by strangers. To state the proposition concisely: *Spenser conceives the Tudor rule as a return of the old British line; he conceives Elizabeth Tudor as the particular sovereign, coming out of Faerie, whose return fulfills the old prophecy.* That is to say, the poem is at once a glorification of Elizabeth's ancestry and a glorification of the Queen as an individual. Had England's greatness in the last two decades of the sixteenth century, Spenser's time, an era which the poet recognized as not only putting the realm on a new footing of prosperity and power but also as marking the beginning of a far-reaching imperial policy,—had this greatness come during the rule of a Tudor king, Spenser would have figured that king under the name of Prince Arthur. But his sovereign was a woman. The prophecy, then, is fulfilled through personifying, in Arthur, the spirit of Great Britain, now united to the Faerie Queene herself. This is not only an excellent poetical device; it is also a most interesting development of the Arthurian legend, true to the spirit of that legend if not to its letter. It is also quite in keeping with Spenser's method of complex allegory, a method by which different qualities and forces, different attributes of perfection, are, like Plato's *ideas,* embodied now in one concrete form and now in another.

These statements are, I think, capable of nearly formal proof. To begin with, there is a sharp distinction, throughout the *Faerie Queene,* between *fairy* knight and British. Thus, Artegal is a changeling, not a fairy:

> He wonneth in the land of Fayeree,
> Yet is no fairy borne, ne sib at all
> To Elfes, but sprong of seed terrestriall,
> And whylom by false fairies stolen away. (3. 3. 26.)

Guyon on the other hand, is " elfin borne "; he was of noble state and " mickle worship in his native land "; he had been knighted by Huon (2. 1. 6). Amphisa was a fairy " by race " (3. 6. 4). Priamond and his brothers were born of a fay (4. 2. 44). Redcross, however, was "sprong out from English race, however now accompted Elfins sonne." The Hermit goes on to explain that he came from the ancient race of Saxon kings, but was stolen as a child by a fairy who left her own child and took Redcross to fairy land where he was brought up by a ploughman. (1. 10. 60-67. Compare the " Birth of St. George," in Percy, and the story of the " weird ladye of the woods." The Hermit tells Redcross that he is to be known as " Saint George of mery England.") Furthermore, Prince Arthur, not a fairy but a " Briton knight," seeks Gloriana, the Fairy Queen, whom he has seen in a vision. Her image he bears on his shield. Guyon, a fairy knight, promises to aid him in his quest, and they are companions throughout the second book. In the House of Alma they read with delight ancient chronicles that set forth the origin of each: Arthur reads *Briton Moniments* and Guyon *Antiquitee of Faery Lond.*

Summarizing the evidence thus far, we note: (1) the careful distinction between the two classes of knights, a distinction that is preserved both for the great knights and for the lesser figures as well. (2) The hero of Book I is a Briton; of Book II is a Fairy. Yet there is no distinction in appearance, size or personal character, the distinction is of race. Both classes of knights perform valorous deeds against enchantment; the Fairy possesses no supernatural power, for example, as against the Briton. (3) Arthur, contrary to certain folk traditions is not a fairy sovereign; Gloriana is.

We come now to a consideration of the place of the chronicles in the *Faerie Queene.* These are found in 2. 10., in which is given a rhymed chronicle of British kings from Brutus to Uther, and in 3. 3., where the history is continued in the form of Merlin's prophecy to Britomart concerning her descendants as far as Cadwallader, last of the kings. Only Arthur and his son are omitted. Miss Carrie M. Harper, in her excellent study of the sources of Spenser's history, has suggested that the British point of view and the interest in Welsh tradition, " may be partly accounted for by the Welsh blood of the Tudors." It is safe to go much farther than this. Far from being mere episodes, these chronicles are important structurally. This is indicated by the elaborate invocations prefixed to the cantos containing the historical material, and also by Spenser's repeated statements that in this poem he is celebrating the ancestry of the Queen. (Compare, for example, 2. Prologue, st. 4, where the English realm is called the " lond of Faery " and in this " antique ymage " the Queen is asked to see her " great auncestry." See also the invocations to 2. 10, and 3. 3.) Moreover, while Spenser's chronicle deals only

with British kings and is thus a recognition of Elizabeth's
British ancestry, the point is driven home by the means of the
fairy chronicle, which is definitely referred to the Tudor house.
Most of the fairy monarchs have the word *elf* incorporated in
their names, from Elfe, the founder of the dynasty, who
wedded a fay, through Elfin (The name Elphin is often met
in Welsh folks tales. One hero of that name was the finder of
the bard Taliessin. See *Mabinogion,* ed. Guest, p. 325; Rhys,
Arthurian Legend, p. 318, etc.), Elfinan, Elfiline, Elfinell,
Elfant, Elfar, Elfinor, down to Elficleos, who is identified
with Henry VII. Oberon (Henry VIII) succeeded, since
Elferon (Prince Arthur) died before his father, and the last
reigning monarch is Tanaquil (Gloriana), by whom Spenser
means Elizabeth. (The passage is in 2. 10. 70 ff. The Welsh
word for Elves is *Ellyllon,* a point not without significance
here.)

By this means Spenser is able to bridge the gap in chronology
necessary to his design; he omits all reference to Saxon or
Norman kings, or to kings of England prior to Henry VII.
The past, both near and remote, is blended with the present.
Arthur and Gloriana are in one sense the ancestors of Elizabeth; in another sense they are now living, rulers of England.
(Thus, for example, in 2. 10. 4 Spenser says that Elizabeth's
name, realm, and race come from Prince Arthur. Here he is
thinking of the historical Arthur, ancestor of Elizabeth in the
literal sense.) This fact may be plainly seen if we add to
these two chronicles the revelation of Britomart's descendants
as given to her by Merlin (3. 3. 26 ff.). Artegal, whom Britomart is to wed, is not a fairy, though he thinks he was born
from the union of an elf with a fay. In truth, Merlin says, he
is son of Gorlois and brother of the Cornish king, Cador.
The name Artegal comes from the chronicles and, as Miss
Harper observes (pp. 143-4), the device makes up for the
omission of the historical Arthur here and in Book II. At

the end of Merlin's list of kings we are told that the Britons will be driven out first by a Raven (the Danes) and then by the Lion of Neustria (William of Normandy), but that " when the term is full accomplished . . . a sparke of fire " shall break forth from Mona and

> So shall the Briton blood their crowne agayn reclame.

(Mona is one of the " Isles of the Dead," like Avalon [Glastonbury], according to Rhys, p. 356. Thus the fairy-return idea comes once more.) Thus Spenser once more covers the period from 1228 when Llewellyn, the last British prince, gave up Wales and retired to Anglesey (Mona), where Henry VII was afterwards born. By this means the chronological interim is bridged, as by the device of the fairy genealogy in 2. 10, and we are once more brought to the Tudor regime.

Preparatory to an interpretation of these facts it is necessary to recall the various aspects under which Elizabeth appears. As Gloriana, she typifies not only the glory but the " rule " of England. (See the *Letter*, the proem to 2. stanzas 4 and 5, and the proem to 3. st. 5.) As Belphoebe and, to a certain extent, as Britomart, she typifies chastity. But as Britomart she is primarily representative of British power, the warlike might of England. (Strictly speaking, the third book deals with the rescue of Amoret. Scudamore, the knight who should be the hero of the book, does not succeed in accomplishing his " adventure," so Britomart comes to his assistance. Thus Britomart is the counterpart of Arthur in the other books, with the difference that while Arthur renders assistance to Redcross and Guyon in their hour of need, each of the titular heroes of the first two books achieves his final " adventure " without any aid from the " greatest knight in the world." It is this well-known romance convention that Spenser makes use of in his poem, not the idea that no one virtue is sufficient but that Magnificence includes them all.) As Mercilla, she is Elizabeth the merciful, the poet's interpretation of her unwillingness to sentence Mary of Scotland to death. She is also, of course, Cynthia, a conception parallel to that of Belphoebe; and Tanaquil, the daughter of Henry VIII. Of all these conceptions, that of Gloriana *plus* Britomart is by far the most constant and important. The union between Arthur and Gloriana and that between Artegal and Britomart then become significant of Spenser's fundamental conception in the structure of the poem. How closely knit the two stories are is indicated by the facts, already pointed out, that Artegal parallels Arthur in an important sense in the chronicles, and that Britomart, in Book III at least, plays Arthur's rôle. The full significance of this conception it is now possible to define.

By *Fairy* Spenser means *Welsh,* or, more accurately, *Tudor,* as distinguished from the general term British. He looks on England as Britain, ignoring, for the purpose of his poem, post-Conquest history. (The words "England" and "English" occur only a few times in the entire *F. Q.* St. George [Redcross] belongs to mery England"; he is sprung from " English race," born of " English blood " [1. 10. 60-64]. The only other examples of the use of the word have nothing to do with what is discussed in this place.) The Tudor dynasty, therefore, brings back the ancient British line, and one purpose of the poem is to celebrate this fact in compliment to the Queen. But Gloriana, the Faerie Queene, is *Elizabeth Tudor.* The old British spirit, the real England, represented in Prince Arthur, finds in her " glory," in the rich connotation given that term in the Renaissance, and also the powerful government (" rule "—see the proem to 3, stanza 5) that was making England a great European power and was the prophecy of the coming British imperialism. Thus the epic celebrates both the ancestry of Elizabeth, the return of the old British strain, and also her greatness as an individual. The title that Spenser chooses for his poem takes on new significance.

It remains only to add that the Britomart-Artegal story relates primarily to Great Britain. The deeds of Artegal, for example, as I have pointed out elsewhere [Ch. IV], reflect the international relations of Elizabeth's government, especially the conflict with Philip of Spain. But the Arthur-Gloriana story, complementary to this, is concerned with the return of the native British race to power. Spenser has left evidence of this distinction in the passage (3. 2. 7-8) in which Britomart says that she has come from her " native soyle, that is by name The greater Britaine," to " Faery lond," where she has heard that many famous knights and ladies dwell. That is, fairy land, for the moment, is Wales, the last stronghold of Britain. This is quite in agreement with the entire conception. Avalon, Fairy Land, Wales, is ruled by a *fée* who became the protector of Arthur, healed his wound, and preserved him until the time for his return, in the Tudor house, to worldly empire. The only addition that Spenser makes is that the great *fée,* in the person of Elizabeth, herself assumes the rule of Great Britain.

FOR CHAPTER II

Page 60.   Miss Lilian Winstanley's edition of Book I of the *Faerie Queene* was published at Cambridge, 1915. See the Introduction.

Page 61.   Professor F. M. Padelford's *The Political and Ecclesiastical Allegory of the First Book of the Faerie Queene* was published at Boston, 1911.   J. E. Whitney's " The Continued Allegory in the First Book of the *Faery Queene* " was published in the *Transactions of the American Philological Association* 19. 40-69.

The Rev. Henry J. Todd's *The Works of Edmund Spenser,* published in 8 volumes in 1805, was the first variorum edition of Spenser.   Sir Walter Scott's review is to be found in the *Edinburgh Review* 7 (1806). 203-217.

A series of studies in this field is now under way in the English Seminary at The Johns Hopkins University. Reference is made in this chapter to Dr. Ray Heffner's investigation of the influence of contemporary masques, pageants, and panegyric verse, in the first book of the *Faerie Queene.* Part of his material Dr. Heffner published in *Studies in Philology* (April, 1930), and he led a discussion of the problem of interpretation at the Washington meeting of the Modern Language Association. In a dissertation presented in May, 1930, Dr. Ivan Schulze discussed the influence of pageantry on the *Faerie Queene,* and in another dissertation, 1928, Dr. Frederick Hard investigated the relations of certain parts of the *Faerie Queene* to tapestries, paintings, and other aspects of Elizabethan art.

Page 62. Thomas Warton's *Observations on the Faerie Queene* was first published in 1754, but a second edition, " corrected and enlarged," was issued in 1762. The reference is from the first edition, p. 219.

Page 63. Upton's edition of the *Faerie Queene* appeared in 2 vols. in 1758; the first reference is to 2. 432. The identification of Henry VIII with Redcross is to be found in the note on *F. Q.* 1. 4. 43 (2. 367) ; the summary of the first book is on 2. 427-8.

Page 64. Dryden's statement is from his *Works,* ed. Scott and Saintsbury, 13. 17.

Page 65. For James's anger with Spenser see the letter of Robert Bowes to Lord Burghley in *CSP, Scotland* 2. 726. A transcript of the original is printed in Carpenter's *Reference Guide,* p. 41.

Ben Jonson's statement that Spenser in a letter to Raleigh identified Mary Stuart as Duessa can be found in Jonson's *Works,* ed. Gifford and Cunningham, 3. 478.

Dr. H. E. Cory's *Edmund Spenser, a Critical Study* was published at Berkeley, 1917. See my review in *MLN* 35 (1920). 165-177.

Page 66. Nashe's conception of poetry is to be found in his *Anatomie of Absurditie* (1589) ; see the extract in Gregory Smith's *Elizabethan Critical Essays* 1. 328. John Harington's *A Preface, or rather a Briefe Apologie of Poetrie* was prefixed to his translation of *Orlando Furioso* (1591) ; reprinted in *Eliz. Crit. Essays* 2. 194-222.

Chapman's position is summed up in his dedication to Mathew Roydon of his *Ovid's Banquet of Sense* (1595) ; it is, of course, stated in many of his Prefaces (especially to the *Odysseys*) and in the poems themselves.

Milton's praise of the *Faerie Queene* is in *Areopagitica;* see my article in *SP* 14. 1-22.

Page 67. Maurice Kyffin in his *Blessednes of Brytaine* (1587) advised:

> Ye Bryttish poets, Repeat in Royall song,
> With waightie words, *used in King Arthurs daies*
> Th' Imperiall Stock, from whence your Queene hath sprong
> Enstall in verse your Princesse lasting prayses.

An earlier stanza begins with this reference to Elizabeth:

> A Blessed Branch of Brutus Royall Race;
> To Brytish Wightes a Blisfull worldly joy.
>   (Quoted from W. C. Hazlitt, ed., *Fugitive Tracts* 1.)

Page 68. G. B. Harrison's explanation of the allegory in the *Avisa* is in the " Essay " appended to his edition, Bodley Head Quartos 15 (1926).

Norman D. Solve's dissertation, *Stuart Politics in Chapman's Tragedy of Chabot,* was published at Ann Arbor, 1928, as vol. 4 of the *Univ. of Michigan Pub. in Lang. and Lit.*

Miss Lilian Winstanley's statement that " Spenser's *Faerie Queene* is really an epic of the religious wars in Europe " is in her *Othello as the Tragedy of Italy* (1924), p. 16. See also p. 128.

Page 70. Ramsay's discussion is in his edition of *Magnyfycence, EETS,* 1906.

Miss Winstanley's *Macbeth, King Lear & Contemporary History* was published at Cambridge, 1922.

Page 76. Miss Edith Rickert's "Political Satire in *A Midsummer Night's Dream*" was printed in *MP* 21 (1923).

Page 80. The topical nature of the allusion to Essex in the prologue to Act 5 of *Henry V* is made apparent by its close resemblance to Stowe's account of Essex's departure for Ireland (*Annales*, 1631, p. 788):

. . . in all which places and in feldes, the people pressed exceedingly to behold him, especially in the high wayes, for more then seven miles space, crying and saying, God blesse your Lordship, God preserve your honour, and some followed him until evening, only to behold him. . . .

Dover Wilson and Quiller-Couch's ed. of *Love's Labour's Lost* was printed at Cambridge, 1923; see the introduction. Compare G. B. Harrison's *An Elizabethan Journal*, 1928, pp. 421-4.

Miss Evelyn May Albright's "Shakespeare's *Richard II* and the Essex conspiracy," *PMLA* 42 (1927). 686-720, was answered by Dr. Ray Heffner in *PMLA* 45. 754-780. That the subject of Richard II was not in itself dangerous is pointed out by Dr. Heffner from the fact that Hayward's *Henry IV* was allowed to circulate, even after it had been called in question, with only the dedication "commanded to be cut out." It contained the desposing of Richard II.

Page 81. For Elizabeth's threat to suppress Holinshed's *Chronicles*, see *CSP, Dom.*, 1581-90, p. 697.

Page 82. Miss Albright's article on *Henry V* is in *PMLA* 43 (1928). 722 ff. She ignores Professor Tucker Brooke's argument against the Essex identification in his *Shakespeare of Stratford* (New Haven, 1925), which seems to me much more convincing than Miss Albright's.

Page 83. I do not, however, share Professor Tucker Brooke's view of Shakespeare as "the man of Stratford," not interested in any of the great questions of his day.

Page 87. Ray Heffner's " Spenser's Allegory in Book I of the *Faerie Queene* " was printed in *SP* for April, 1930.

Page 89. Burghley's account of the masque to be presented before Elizabeth and Mary is in *Lansdowne MS* 5; cited by Reyher *Les Masques Anglais*, pp. 125 ff.

Page 93. Elizabeth's own recognition of Temperance as a political virtue is to be found in *The Copie of a Letter to the Right Honourable the Earle of Leycester . . . with a report of certaine petitions and declarations made to the Qveenes Maiestie at two seuerall times, from all the Lordes and Commons lately assembled in Parliament. And her Maiesties answeres thereunto by herselfe deliuered . . . Imprinted at London by Christopher Barker, Printer to the Queenes most excellent Maiestie. 1586.* She says:

When first I tooke the Scepter, my title made me not forget the giuer: and therefore began, as it became me, with such religion, as both I was borne in, bred in, & I trust shal die in. Although I was not so simple, as not to know what danger and perill so great an alteration might procure: howe many great Princes of the contrary opinion woulde attempt all they might against me: and generally, what enimitie I shoulde breede vnto my selfe: which all I regarded not, knowing that he, for whose sake I did it, might, and would defend me. For which it is, that euer since I have bene so daungerously prosecuted, as I rather maruaile that I am, then muse that I should not be: if it were not Gods holy hand that continueth me, beyond all other expectation. . . .

Then entred I further into the schoole of experience, bethinking what it fitted a King to do: and there I saw, he scant was wel furnished, if either he lacked Justice, Temperance, Magnanimitie, or Judgement. As for the two latter, I wil not boaste, my sexe doeth not permit it: But for the two first, this dare I say, Amongst my subiects I neuer knew a difference of person, where right was one: Nor neuer to my knowledge preferred for favour, whome I thought not fit for worth: Nor bent my eares to credit a tale that first was told me: Nor was so rash, to corrupt my iudgement with my censure, before I heard the cause. (pp. 30-31)

Nichols (1. 28) cites Camden to the effect that Edward VI

used to call Elizabeth his "sweet sister Temperance." Certainly her course on coming to the throne was, as she herself says, a temperate one. Her situation was delicate; many of her subjects were Catholic and hostile to any change, and her problem was further complicated by Mary Stuart's claim to the throne. This she recognized, as we see in the following passage, which Nichols (*Progresses* 1. 20) quotes from Strype's *Annals* (2. 88):

Queen Elizabeth would sometimes, in the midst of her cares, divert herself by study and sometimes versifying, as she did in composing a copy of verses upon the Queen of Scots, and those of her friends here in England near this time; which Dr. Wylson hath preserved to us in his English Logic. For she, to declare that she was nothing ignorant of those secret practices among her people, and many of her Nobility inclining too far to the Scottish Queen's party, though she had long with great wisdom and patience dissembled it (as the said Dr. Wylson prefaceth her verses), wrote this ditty most sweet and sententious; not hiding from all such aspiring minds the danger of their ambition and disloyalty. Which afterwards fell out most truly, by the exemplary chastisement of sundry persons, who, in favour of the said Scottish Queen, declining from her Majesty, sought to interrupt the quiet of her realm, by many evil and undutiful practises. Her verses were as follow:

That doubt of future foes exiles my present joy;
And Wit me warns to shun such snares, as threaten mine annoy.
For falsehood now doth flow, and subjects' faith doth ebb:
Which would not be, if Reason rul'd, or Wisdom weav'd the webb.
But clouds of toys untry'd do cloak aspiring minds,
Which turn to rain of late repent, by course of changed winds.
The top of Hope suppos'd the root of truth wil bee,
And fruitless al their graffed guiles, as shortly ye shal see.
Those dazzled eyes with pride, which great Ambition blinds,
Shal be unseel'd by worthy wights, whom Foresight falsehood finds.
The daughter of debate, that eke Discord doth sow,
Shal reap no gain, where former rule hath taught still peace to grow.
No foreign banisht Wight shal anchor in this port:
Our realm it brooks no strangers force: let them elsewhere resort.
Our rusty sword with rest shal first the edge employ,
To poll their topps that seek such change, and gape for joy.

The notes to the poem (by Strype or Nichols) identify "Ambition" as the Duke of Norfolk; "Wight" as the Scottish Queen; and "strangers" as France and Spain. Note the Queen's consciousness of danger through ambition and disloyalty, and, in this connection, Guyon's successful resistance to such temptation. Her poem was well known, because it was printed by Wilson, and it uses an allegory in which well known figures appear. It could, therefore, be understood by everyone. The emphasis on the rule of Reason threatened by falsehood, ambition, "clouds of toys," all suggest the philosophical background of Book II of the *Faerie Queene*. The enemies are daughter of debate, Discord, and outside enemies.

All this strengthens our interpretation of Book II as dealing with Elizabeth's right to the throne and the threats made against that right. After the settlement of the problem of religion, the danger from the Scottish Queen was fundamental. She was indeed an Acrasia. Miss Winstanley (*Othello*, p. 39) identifies her with Acrasia on the basis of John Knox's reference to her as a mermaid, enticing men by her beauty and her flattering songs. Her influence over Norfolk and her partial seduction of Leicester, Sir Henry Sidney, and others of the English court, lend weight to such a characterization.

This explains how Guyon could be prepared by reading chronicles for the overthrow of Acrasia. He is closely associated with Arthur at this time and finds in the Chronicles Elizabeth's right to the throne, because of her descent from the ancient "Briton line." The histories prepare him, therefore, for the overthrow of an enchantress presumably working against Elizabeth's claim. This enchantress is Mary of Scotland.

Page 95. Dr. William Haller's "Before *Areopagitica*" was published in *PMLA* 42. 875 ff.

Page 98. Arthur first tells his vision of the Faerie Queene and his "lignage" in Book I (canto 9, stanzas 3-17).

In a note to Song X of the *Polyolbion*, (Chalmers ed. p.

254), Selden cites this passage in reference to Merlin. Todd quotes this, in abbreviated form, but apparently no editor gets the distinction between the two Merlins. Selden's note reads:

In the first declining state of the British empire (to explain the author in this of Merlin) Vortigern, by advice of his magicians, after divers unfortunate successes in war, resolved to erect a strong fort in Snowden hills (not far from Conway's head, in the edge of Merioneth) which might be his last and surest refuge against the increasing power of the English. Masons were appointed, and the work begun; but what they built in the day, was always swallowed up in the earth next night. The king asks council of his magicians touching this prodigy: they advise, that he must find out a child which had no father, and with his blood sprinkle the stones and mortar, and that then the castle would stand as on a firm foundation. Search was made, and in Caer-Merdhin (as you have it to the fifth song) was Merlin Ambrose found: he, being hither brought to the king, slighted that pretended skill of those magicians, as palliated ignorance; and with confidence of a more knowing spirit undertakes to show the true cause of that amazing ruin of the stonework; tells them, that in the earth was a great water, which could endure continuance of no heavy super-structure. The workmen digged to discover the truth, and found it so. He then beseeches the king to cause them make farther inquisition, and affirms, that in the bottom of it were two sleeping dragons; which proved so likewise, the one white, the other read; the white he inter-preted for the Saxons, the red for the Britons: and upon this event here in Dinas Emrys (Ambrose's Bury, Itinerar. 2. c. 8) as they call it, began he those prophecies to Vortigern, which are common in the British story. Hence questionless was that fiction of the Muses' best pupil, the noble Spenser (Faery Q. lib. i. Cant. 9. Stanz. 4) in suppos-ing Merlin usually to visit his old Timonm whose dwelling he places

> low in a valley green,
> Under the foot of Rauran mossy hoar
> From whence the river Dee as silver cleen,
> His tumbling billows rolls with gentle roar.

For this Rauran-vaur hill is thereby in Merioneth: but observe withal, the difference of the Merlins, Ambrose, and Silvester, which is before to the fourth song; and permit it only as poetical, that he makes king Arthur and this Merlin of one time. These prophecies were by

Geffrey ap Arthur at request of Alexander, Bishop of Lincoln, under Henry I turned into Latin, and some three hundred years since had interpretation bestowed on them by a German doctor, one Alanus de Insulis, who never before, but twice since that unhappy inauguration and mighty increase of dominion in our present sovereign, that been imprinted.

An earlier instance in Selden's *Illustrations* (Song VIII, ed. Chalmers, 231) refers to be supposed prophecy of Merlin:

> Doctrinae studium quod nunc viget ad vada Boum
> Ante finem secli celebrabitur ad vada Saxi

"Which you shall have englished in that solemnized marriage of Thames and Medway, by a most admired Muse of our nation, thus with advantage." Then he cites, and quotes, *F. Q.* 4. 11. 35 and glosses " Holland " in Spenser as " The maritime part of Lincolnshire, where, Welland a river."

Page 102. Heywood's story of Edward VI is told in his *Englands Elizabeth* (ed. 1631), p. 64.

FOR CHAPTER III

Page 104. Spenser's letter to Harvey is cited from Grosart's *Works of Harvey* 1. 6 ff.

Page 106. The quotations are from the same source, pp. 7, 17, and 16. Spenser also (p. 7) advises Harvey to look out for preferment for himself: " And indeede for your self to, it sitteth with you now, to call your wits and senses togither . . . when occasion is so fairely offered of Estimation Preferment. For, whiles the yron is hote, it is good striking, and minds of Nobles varie, as their Estates." Harvey's reply dated Oct. 23, chaffs Spenser on this business-like manner and wagers all the books in his study that Spenser will not go over sea by next week or the week after. Harvey was evidently skeptical of his friend's enthusiasm.

Page 107. The "Three Proper . . . letters" are cited from Harvey's *Works,* ed. Grosart, 1. 29 ff.

Page 109. Talbot is quoted from Nares, *Memoir of Burghley* 3, 114. Castelnau's letter is quoted from Hume's *Courtships of Queen Elizabeth,* pp. 207-8.

Page 110. Sidney's letter was written in January, 1588, and Sir Philip was excluded from the royal presence for a time, as a punishment.

Burghley's famous letter to the Queen, under date of 28 Jan., 1580, is in *Hatfield House Records,* 2. 308-310. In it he states that he had favored the marriage as one that would make for her honor and safety and enable her to "rule the Sternes of the shippes of Europe with more fame than ever came to any Quene of the Wordell." Now that the negotiations are off, it is his duty to point out the dangers of Elizabeth's position with reference to the Powers, and to suggest ways and means. He then gives an alarming list of dangers, proposing some measures which, he confesses, are but "shews of remedies," "whereas her marriage, if she had liked it, myght have provided her more surety with less peril." If we take all this literally, it reveals that Burghley actually favored the marriage. But the man was as crafty as Elizabeth herself, and we cannot be sure that this is not mere rhetoric, delivered after he felt that the real danger was past. That the court, however, believed Burghley to favor the match, I think there is not the smallest doubt.

Page 112. In a letter of 29 January, 1580, Simier begs Elizabeth to protect him from the fury of the bear: "Qu'il vous playse le conserver de la pate de l'ours" (*Hatfield House* 2. 311). This seems to refer to the quarrel with Leicester. Camden (*Elizabeth,* English translation, ed. 1635, p. 205) reports:

In the meane while, Simier ceased not amorously to wooe Queene Elizabeth, and though she stifly refused the marriage a long time, yet hee drew her to that passe, that Leicester (who from his heart opposed the marriage) and others, spred rumours abroad, that by amorous potions and unlawfull arts he had crept into the Queenes minde, and inticed her to the love of Aniou. And Simier on the other side left no meanes unassayed to remove Leicester out of place and grace with the Queene, revealing unto her his marriage with Essex his widdow: whereat the Queene grew into such a chafe, that she commanded Leicester to keepe himselfe within the Tower of Greenwich, and thought to have committed him to the Tower of London, which his enemies much desired. But Sussex, though his greatest and heaviest adversary, who wholly bent himselfe to set forward the marriage with Aniou, disswaded her, whilest out of a sound judgment and the in-nated generousnesse of his noble minde, he held opinion that no man was to be molested for lawfull Marriage, which amongst all men hath ever beene honest and honoured. Yet glad he was that by this marriage he was now out of all hope of marrying with the Queene. Neverthelesse, Leicester was so incensed herewith, that he bent himselfe to revenge the wrong he had received. And there wanted not some, which accused him, as if he had suborned one Teuder of the Queenes guard, an hackster, to take away Simiers life. Certainely the Queene commanded by publique Proclamation, that no man should wrong Simier, his companions or servants, in word or deed. At which time it happened, that while the Queene for her pleasure was rowed in her Barge upon the Thames neere Greenwich, with Simier, the Earle of Lincolne, and Hatton her Vice-chamberlaine, a young man, dis-charged a Piece out of a Boat, and shot one of the Bargemen in the Queenes Barge thorow both his armes: who was soone apprehended and led to the Gallowes for a terrour to him: but whereas he religiously affirmed that hee did it unwittingly, and thought no harme, he was dis-charged. Neither would the Queene beleeve that which some buzzed in her eares, that he was purposely suborned against her or Simier. So farre was she from giving way to suspition against her people, that she was many times wont to say: That She could beleeve nothing of her people, which Parents would not beleeve of their Children.

Nichols (*Progresses* 2. 337 n) holds that Leicester's marriage was no secret to the Queen, for he says, " she was present at the Earls wedding." He cites (p. 223) Churchyard's *A Discourse of the Queenes Majesties Entertainment in Suffolk and Norfolk* . . . [1578] to show that the Queene ended her progress at Wansted House, where on September 20 Leicester married the Dowager of Essex, " in the presence of the Earls of Pembroke and Warwick, and Sir Francis Knolles, his chaplain Mr. Tindal performing the ceremony " (Nichols's statement). He then quotes Churchyard: " And to knit up all, the good chere was revived, not only with making a great feast to the Queene and the French Ambassador, but also in feasting solemnely (at severall times) the whole garb, on Sunday and Munday before the Queene came, at his own table, using such courtesie unto them for the space of two dayes, as was and is worthy of perpetuall memoire.—"

It seems to me that Nichols's conclusions are quite unwarranted: Churchyard does not say that the Queen was at Wanstead House at the time of Leicester's marriage. No mention whatever is made of the marriage in Churchyard's account, as printed in Holinshed (continued by John Stow, ed. 1808, 4. 404).

Simier's complete code is in *Hatfield House* 2. 448.

Page 113. The letters quoted are from *Hatfield House* 2. pp. 311, 314, 318, and 283 respectively. They are all from the latter part of the year 1579-80.

Page 114. The reference to Catherine de Medici as " Mad. de la Serpente " is from *Hatfield House* 2. 30. Alençons reference to " nostre singe " is from the same, p. 355. The reference of Simier to himself as " vostre singe " is from the same source, pp. 349-352.

Page 115. Evidence that *Mother Hubberds Tale* was called in is found in Harvey's *Foure Letters* (1592). Harvey says (Grosart's ed., *Works* 1. 164) that " Mother Hubbard, in heat of choller . . . wilfully overshot her malcontented selfe . . ." and he refers again (p. 205) to the " invective and satyricall sprites," who " can tell parlous tales of beares and foxes as shrewdlye as Mother Hubbard, for her life."

Nashe in his *Strange Newes* (1593) replies to Harvey and

attacks him for bringing in Mother Hubbard and so rekindling the displeasure against Spenser. To Harvey, he says reproachfully (*Works,* ed. Grosart, 2. 212) : " Who publikely accusde of late brought *Mother Hubbard* into question that thou shouldst by rehearsall rekindle against him the sparkes of displeasure that were quenched? " (See also the allusion on 2. 270.)

We should add to these the statement in Thomas Scot's *Philomythie* (1616) on the danger of writing in verse which may be given a political application; in the "Address to the Reader," he says:

> The ghost of Virgil's Gnat would not sting so,
> That great men durst not in the City go . . .
> If Spencer now were living to report
> His Mother Hubbert's Tale, there would be sport;
> To see him in a blanket tost and mounted
> Up to the starres. . . .
>   (From Carpenter's *Reference Guide,* p. 249)

This evidence of the calling in of *Mother Hubberds Tale* is discussed by Collier in his *Poetical Decameron* 1. 100; by Sir Israel Gollancz in the *Proceedings of Brit. Academy,* 1907-8, pp. 99-105; and summarized in Cory's *Edmund Spenser* (1917), p. 199.

Grosart (*Works of Spenser* 1. 82) mentions Bacon as another example of a " forward youth " whom Burghley " as was his mode " wished to " keep down." Grosart refers the passage about Leicester's quarrel with the Queen to her discovery of his marriage, but quotes Camden, not noting that Elizabeth got her knowledge from Simier (p. 83). But this, as will appear presently, is not without significance.

Page 118. On the relations of *Mother Hubberds Tale* to the Renard Cycle, see my discussion in *MP,* January, 1905.

Page 119. Mendoza wrote, 8 April, 1579, that Burghley was not so much opposed to the match as formerly, but that he suspects the reason lies in the desire of Burghley and Sussex to bring about the fall of Leicester (cited by Hume, *The Great Lord Burghley*, p. 330, n. 1). In the following March, Leicester, out of favor, told Mendoza that his enemies were plotting the marriage only to spite him (*ib.*, p. 340).

It is said that Stubbs was well acquainted with Spenser. Moreover, Spenser and Sidney were much in each other's company, and at Leicester House, during this time.

Page 121. References to the Plague are numerous at this time. Sir William Fleetwood, Recorder of London, writes to Burghley in October, 1578, that he has been in Buckinghamshire since Michaelmas because he was troubled every day with such as came having plague sores about them, or being sent by the Lords to places where he found dead corpses under the tables, which surely did greatly amaze him (*Hatfield House*, 2. 222). Letters from Paris in 1579-80 report that all study has ceased and friends from England are advised not to travel; importations of certain goods from France were forbidden (*Cal. State Papers, Eliz. Domestic*, 1. 683). Other letters appeal for aid, since the dearth of all things, due to the Plague, renders the need extreme (*State Papers, Eliz.*, 1. 635). Additional instances might be cited.

Simier's influence over the Queen is cited from Nares, *Memoirs of Burghley* 3. 164. This is closely parallel to a passage in *MHT* describing the arts of the false courtier. Ample illustrations might be drawn, if necessary, from the extraordinary letters to and from the Queen.

Alençon's character is quoted from Nares, 3. 183. The account of the Progress of 1578 is cited by Nares, 3. 109, 113, 114 (Topcliff to the Earl of Shrewsbury).

Page 122. Burghley's increased unpopularity about 1591 is summarized in Hume's *The Great Lord Burghley*, pp. 444-450, with the notes.

The reference in the *Ruines of Time* is to lines 449-455.

The deposition of 1592 is cited by Hume, *Great Lord Burghley*, p. 456. For the trouble over Burghley's farming of the customs, see Nares, *Memoirs of Burghley* 3. 372-3.

Dr. Fred Hard has recently (*SP* 28. 219-234) shown that the strictures upon the corrupt ministry of the Fox (lines 1171-1182) may have direct reference to Burghley. The first charge, that by increasing his own income under the guise of increasing " the common treasurer's store," the Fox was enabled to build for himself great mansions, seems a reference to the building of Theobalds by Burghley and Holdenby by Hatton. The second charge, that " other peeres, for povertie were forst their auncient houses to let lie," etc., has reference to offenses committed with Burghley's knowledge and without his censure, if not, indeed, under his sponsorship.

Page 125. In the State Papers (*CSP, Dom.* 1579, p. 634) there are eleven copies of the circular to the Bishops. Some of these are fully signed, some partially, some not signed at all.

For Sidney's punishment, see Fox Bourne, *Life of Sidney*, p. 185. The quarrel with Oxford is told in detail in Fulke Greville's *Life of Sidney* (1652).

Page 126. See Lord Burghley's letter telling of his exclusion from the conference, and the fiery reply of Sussex, in *Hatfield House* 2. 329. The affair between Sussex and Leicester is told in *CSP, Dom.* 2. 22. Leicester's letters are in *State Papers, Domestic,* 1580 (*Cal.* 1. 666, 672).

Page 127. Alençon's letter is from *Hatfield House* 2. 355. Hatton's letter of September, 1580, in from *CSP, Dom.* 1. 677. But that Hatton was insincere is shown by the fact that when, early in 1582, Leicester was forced to accompany Alençon to Brabant, the " sheep " promptly reported a chance remark of the Queen's, with the result that Leicester came post-haste to England, to be called a knave and a traitor for his pains.

The draft of the Act of 1581 is in *CSP, Dom.* 2. 3. For

additional indication of how Leicester was looked upon by the Puritans as their one hope, see the letter to him from Sir Francis Knollys, June, 1580, objecting fiercely to the proposed triumph of Catholicism, plotted out by the *serpentine subtlety* of the Queen Mother's head (*Calendar*, 1. 658).

Page 128. I hardly dare go so far as to suggest that even the snake of the *Gnat* recalls the name by which Catherine was known: " Mad. la Serpente "; yet it seems not impossible. Of course Spenser is following the pseudo-Vergilian *Culex*.

Page 131. The Belphoebe-Timias episode is from *F. Q.* 3. 5. 50; the Amoret incident is in *F. Q.* 4. 7. 35-47; 4. 8. 1 ff.

FOR CHAPTER IV

Page 133. Harvey's letter is from his *Letter Book* (p. 66), ed. E. J. L. Scott for the Camden Society, 1884.

Page 134. Lyly's allegory is discussed by Professor Tucker Brooke, *MLN* 26. 13. In Gascoigne's masque it is shown that Diana lost Zabeta (Elizabeth) years before and now finds her still a virgin though a queen; she begs her not to marry, but Iris, coming from Juno entreats her not to listen to Diana, since it is possible for her in this place where she has passed a pleasant day to enjoy " a world of wealth is wedded state " and there withal to " uphold the staff of her estate." Thus plainly did the earl plan to tell the Queen that by marriage with him she would make her position secure; moreover, a son was promised her. But apparently Elizabeth left somewhat abruptly and the masque was not presented, though Gascoigne tells us everything was ready, every actor in his garment, two or three days before she left. Therefore, Gascoigne was in the service of Leicester in 1575, as Spenser was four years later; it was the habit of the great earl to make use of poets to further his personal ambitions.

Page 141. Letters showing the jealousy and malice of the English leaders are in the *Carew Papers,* February, 1581.

Spenser is not complimentary to the intelligence of the com-
mon people (stanzas 33, 48, 51, 52), who are of the type of
the rabble in Ibsen's *Brand.* The giant is a demagogue who
has ideas about communism and proposes to set right the world.
But to his questions about the mysteries of the universe
Artegall makes the same reply that God made to Job. See
Professor F. M. Padelford's articles in *JEGP* 12 and 14, and
SP 15.

Page 142. For Northumberland's claim of treasure see
Pollard's *Political History of England, 1547-1603,* pp. 278 ff.
The refusal of Parliament to sanction the Queen's claims is
discussed by Pollard, p. 282.

Page 147. That the blatant beast is Scandal is indicated
by a passage in the *Return from Parnassus,* (Arber ed., p. 69) :
" We are fully bent to be Lords of misrule in the world's wide
heath: our voyage is to the Ile of Dogges, there where the
blatant beast doth rule and reigne, Renting the credit of whom
it please."

Page 148. Spenser indorsed his *Veue* " finyss 1596 " and
it must have been written very near that time. There is a
sarcastic reference to Stanihurst (Globe ed., pp. 632, 633),
whose *Plaine and Perfect Description of Ireland* was published
in 1586. The reference to the founding of the " new college "
indicates a date later than 1591, perhaps later than 1593
(Morley, *Ireland under Elizabeth and James,* p. 128). Probably Spenser wrote about 1595-96, when the fickleness of the
government policy had driven men who had to live in the
country nearly to distraction. There is a MS dialogue in the
Irish State Papers, 1598, which purports to be the work of one
Thomas Wilson and is dedicated to Essex. The interlocutors
are Peregryn and Silvyn, suggesting Spenser's two sons, and
the style is similar to that of the *Veue* (Bagwell, *Ireland under
the Tudors,* 3. 302).

My article, " The Influence of Machiavelli on Spenser," was published in *MP*, October, 1909.

Derricke's poem was reprinted at Edinburgh, 1883; see pp. 56 ff. and 65 ff.

Harvey's letter to Spenser is quoted from Gregory Smith's *Elizabethan Critical Essays* 1. 126.

Page 149. The citations from Campion are from Ware's ed. (1633), pp. 25, 28 ff. The dialogue on snakes is cited from Holinshed *Chronicles* (ed. 1808) 6. 10 ff. Spenser's comparison of Irish words with Chaucer's is found in the Globe ed., pp. 639b, 676b. Hooker's account is cited from Holinshed, *Chronicles* 6. 229-232.

Page 151. Russell's advice to capture Tyrone and put him to death is cited from Bagwell, *Ireland Under the Tudors* 3. 261-274.

Page 152. The letter to Burghley is cited from Devereux, *Lives and Letters of the Earls of Essex* 1. 75. Sidney's government in Ireland and his desire to be relieved is discussed by Innes, *England Under the Tudors,* p. 312.

Page 153. Sir John Davies is quoted from Morley's ed. of his *Discoverie of the State of Ireland,* pp. 218, 228. Thomas Lee is quoted from *Desiderata Curiosa Hibernica* (Dublin, 1772) 1. 117, 137.

Page 154. Spenser lived in an age marked by cruelty and reflects the character of his time. Sir Humphrey Gilbert, a man of noble ideals, God-fearing, learned, valiant, had no mercy for the victims of war. Sir Henry Sidney, a man of similar type, suppressed the insurrection in Munster by the same barbarities as marked Smerwick. Raleigh aided Grey at Smerwick; Grey merely followed the orders of the Queen, and was at first rebuked by the Queen not for the slaughter but for sparing the principals. Moreover, it must be remembered that the tragedy at Smerwick came about in consequence of the landing of an enemy's forces on English territory, and that this enemy was making war not honorably but by the methods of a sneak and a coward. This is as good a place as any to point out the extreme smallness of some of the charges brought against Spenser, such as the carp against his objection to mantles and what he says about the bards. As for the mantles, cf. Davies (ed. Morley), p. 335; and also the curious entry in the Dublin Assembly Roll, 1594, 2. 274, in which the wearing of mantles was forbidden; besides, who could wish to lose the sardonic humor of the reply of Eudoxus to Irenaeus (Globe ed., p. 632a). As to the bards, contemporary testimony is with Spenser as to the way in which they fomented strife. Of course, it seems a trifle hard that a poet should advise the extermination of brother poets, however richly they may merit destruction; it depends on the point of view, however. To some people, moving-picture shows make for vice and immorality, while to others they are noble instruments for the development of aesthetic appreciation among our " lower " classes.

Campion is cited from Simpson, *Life of Edmund Campion,* pp. 243-4.

Page 155. For the promise of a million crowns to Philip, see Blunt, *Reformation in England*, 2. 458. Compare also the letter of November 6, 1577, from Sanders to Allen (*Domestic Cal., 1547-80,* p. 565) in which it is said that the pope would send two thousand men to Ireland, " the state of Christendom dependeth on the stout assailing of England." That Leicester was convinced of the danger, perhaps in part by Spenser, is shown by his letter of September 5, 1582 (*Domestic Cal., 1581-90,* p. 69): " Her majesty is slow to believe that the great increase of Papists is of danger to the realm. The Lord of His mercye open her eyes! " Largely through Walsingham and Leicester the reprisals on the Catholics were heavy; Grey, following orders from London destroyed the Italian and Spanish forces at Smerwick in 1580; Campion reported the next year that the prisons were full of Catholics; heavy penalties were prescribed in the act of 1581 " To retaine the Queen's majesty's subjects in their due obedience "; Campion was executed and Parsons, styled a " lurking wolf," was driven out. Of course it is true that some of this zeal was because of the money to be seized from the Catholics; see the note (*Domestic Cal.*, p. 566) about one William Meredith, " an horrible Papiste, and esteemed to be worth fifty pounds."

The description of Sir Henry Sidney in his family life is from Holinshed's *Chronicles* (ed. 1808) 6. 401. It would be easy to multiply examples of the strong Puritan element, almost precisely like that of the seventeenth century, in the chronicles and letters dealing with the Irish question. Without doubt, many Puritans settled there. But Pollard (*Political History,* p. 418) is wrong in saying that Burghley once suggested Ireland as a resort for Puritans, desiring to rid England of a trouble-some faction. He refers to the discussion on the " present state of the realm of England," an abstract of which is found in *Domestic Cal., Addenda, 1566-79,* p. 439; these proposals advised the association of the nobility and others in a society for the defense of the gospel and preservation of the state and the Queen's person; the formation of a society of one hundred " gentlemen of religion " for five years to have charge of three thousand men " in case of peril "; the sending of such Pro-testants as did not like the Queen's form of religion to Ireland, thus delivering the realm from the " precise ministers and their followers." Burghley indorsed this as a " Discourse sent from Tho. Cecil to me. wryten by Mr. Carleton . . . to suffer the precise sort to inhabit Ireland." But he makes no comment on it.

Page 156. The quotation from Hooker is from Holinshed, *op. cit.,* 6. 369. Other illustrations of the biblical influence upon Hooker's style are found at pp. 383, 460, etc., and in his dedication. This subject merits consideration from students of English prose style in the sixteenth century.

Pages 157-8. The quotation is from *F. Q.* 7. 7. 35. The *Veue* is quoted from the Globe edition of Spenser's *Works*, pp. 646a, 621a, 680a, 609a, 656a, 658a, 616b.

Page 159. The quotation is from *F. Q.* 7. 6. 38. As is well known, these cantos on mutability perhaps refer to the constant changes in the English policy, which prolonged the struggle. That Spenser here and in the *Veue* was in exact accord with so capable and farsighted a man as Raleigh is seen in the account of Raleigh by Edwards (1. 104): "He was often called into council in relation to these affairs of State and Government in Ireland, and was always of one mind about them. His face was set, as flint, against piddling interferences and temporizing expedients in dealing with great evils. To cut the tap root, rather than to spend precious time in pruning the branches, was his maxim." It is also worth noting that in this respect of strong medicine both Raleigh and Spenser differed from Burghley, as they differed from him in other points. See Burghley's letter to the Queen, *Hatfield House,* 2. 308-10, in which he advised extreme mildness.

Pages 159-160. For the facts on which this summary of English policy is based see Innes, *op. cit.,* pp. 375-383; Pollard, *op. cit.,* pp. 414 ff.

Page 161. Drake is characterized as an ocean knight-errant by Innes, *op. cit.,* p. 347.

Pages 161-2. Fulke Greville's *Life of Sidney* is cited from the reprint of the first edition by the Caradoc Press, pp. 32, 33, 62, 65, 67, 70, 76, 78, 81-5, 88, 89. It will be remembered that Sidney was sent to Holland to prevent him from accompanying Drake.

Page 163. Gilbert's study of navigation is from Hooker (Holinshed, 6. 368). Raleigh's "Maxims of State" is cited from the Oxford ed. of the *Complete Works* 8. 1 ff. Compare also his *The Cabinet Council, Containing the Chief Arts of Empire and Mysteries of State,* published by Milton.

Spenser's stanza about "hardy enterprize" is in *F. Q.* 5. 4. 19. "Many great regions are discovered" is from *F. Q.* 2. pr. 2. The stanza quoted is from *F. Q.* 6. 12. 1.

Page 164. For the calling in of Drayton's version of the Psalms, see Sheavyn, *Literary Profession in the Elizabethan Age,* p. 45.

Page 165. Artegal's censure of Burbon is quoted from *F. Q.* 5. 11. 56.